Contents

Preface

What must Londoners have thought in 1483 when two little medieval celebrities, the most famous children in all of England, dropped out of sight? How long did it take people to notice that twelve-year-old Edward Plantagenet and his ten-year-old brother, Richard, the sons of the late King Edward IV, hadn't been seen in public for a while? When did the subject of foul play come up?

We can do little more than imagine. No fifteenth-century paparazzi haunted the gates of the Tower of London, eager to capture the boys' images through a carriage window. No columnists or bloggers counted the days since little Edward and Richard last were seen. Surely people talked—people always talk—but what did they say?

History can teach us all kinds of useful things if we bother to pay attention. Its rich, intertwining narratives are chock-full of lessons about how and how not to behave in the world. It can teach the alert politician about wooing an electorate. It offers countless examples of wars, how they can (and usually do) go wrong and why they are best avoided. It teaches that even the most super of superpowers can (and usually does) overreach and that every empire inevitably crumbles

All of which is incredibly valuable—again, if you're paying attention. But this book isn't about all that. It's about another facet of history—that shiny, reflective side that invites you to imagine yourself in the picture, to speculate about what it must have felt like to stand shivering in the cold pre–dawn alongside the smoldering rubble of Kirk o'Field in Edinburgh in the wee morning hours of February 10, 1567. Isn't that the sulfurous stench of burnt gunpowder I smell? Who could have blown the place to bits? What happened to the people inside? Where is the king? Did the queen have something to do with this?

This book is about the wondering. For all of history's raw data—dates, documents, detritus—history remains at its heart a realm of mystery. We can read about it, memorize the details, accept or challenge the judgments of historians, but even when the facts are reasonably complete, we can't really *know* the past. And when facts are lacking, we fall back on imagining the mood within Tutankhamen's palace in 1327 BCE Egypt as the young king lay dying. We stand a far better chance of imagining ourselves in a limousine speeding into a Paris tunnel on a summer night in 1997, but even then we cannot be certain of what transpired as the car carrying Princess Diana veered out of control, whether she screamed as it entered its final, fatal skid.

When hard information is incomplete, we can't help but invent missing pieces. What really happened to the little princes in the Tower of London? It's possible that they survived. Maybe they lived long lives, maybe even happy ones. But nobody really thinks so. And the story as it has been most often told—a luridly imagined tale of calculated, politically motivated child murder by their royal uncle, a power–mad misfit—makes their story a natural for this book.

Who really conspired to blow up Scotland's young king Richard Darnley in 1567? Was his wife Mary, Queen of Scots, a murderess? Did Britain's royal family stalk Princess Di? Add to unanswered questions and unknowable motives the tantalizing fact that the main characters of the following chapters were princes, kings, queens, and other royals, and you have what I like to think is an irresistible allure. Long predating modern celebrity, royalty has always been the object of fascination and fantasy. Vicarious glory, national pride, prurient obsession, and—in the pre–democratic era—good old–fashioned fear have always made royals even more absorbing to wonder about than movie stars are today.

The Plantagenet princes, after all, represented not just box-office numbers but the fate of a nation. Little Edward Plantagenet had briefly reigned (in name at least) as King Edward V, before his uncle, the notorious Richard III, nudged him aside. That's the biggest reason why Uncle Richard remains the case's prime suspect

Today's celebrity–sodden media often has to make do with turning the lives of movie stars into mysteries: Will Katie Holmes stick with husband Tom Cruise or will his rigid devotion to Scientology drive her away? Is serial adopter Angelina Jolie a great humanitarian or a self–promoter? But these are lightweight matters compared to the conniving, often treacherous, always high–stakes lives of royalty through history. Although Princess Di may have looked like glamorous tabloid fodder (which she was), and although U.K. royalty wields but little of the actual political power it once did, Diana's sudden death triggered scattershot accusations that have rattled against the protective armor of respected intelligence agencies and even a prime minister. For a movie-star death to merit such speculation, you'd have to throw in a political sex scandal. (Think Marilyn Monroe, a U.S. president, and his attorney general brother.) My point is that royalty trumps mere celebrity.

I wish I could say that for these reasons I dreamed up the idea behind this book. However, I must bow to Paul Aron, author of previous *Unsolved Mysteries* volumes. Also to Stephen Power at Wiley, who gave me a chance to follow in Aron's footsteps. I hope the reader gets as much fun out of it as I have.

Introduction

Napoléon Bonaparte once commented that his life was like a novel. Following that comparison, his last years—1815 to 1821—comprise the sad epilogue. The defeated and deposed French emperor—an unwilling guest of the British government on an island outpost in the South Atlantic Ocean—licked his psychic wounds and chafed at his powerlessness while his health steadily declined.

For many of his worshipful French contemporaries, Napoleon's adventurous and complicated life was one of those novels that a reader hates to see end. They hoped for another comeback like the one that the emperor had pulled off—for a while, anyway—in 1814. After Napoleon's enemies forced him to abdicate and shipped him to the island of Elba, in the Mediterranean Sea, Napoleon confounded those foes by escaping exile, reassembling his loyal troops, and reclaiming power for a frantic three months. Then on June 18, 1815, combined British,

Belgian, Dutch, and Prussian troops outfought Napoleon's army near the village of Waterloo, Belgium—the general's final defeat.

Supporters imagined that their hero could escape exile again, perhaps even seize the throne in Paris once more. There were a number of reasons, however, why Napoleon could not do that. The biggest obstacle was the British. After forcing Napoleon to abdicate for the second time, they did not return him to Elba but installed him instead on the island of St. Helena, a geographically isolated stopping-off place for transatlantic shipping. There the local British authorities watched the former emperor and his household (servants and companions) carefully to ensure that he was not secreted aboard a cargo ship bound for Calais—or Argentina, for that matter. Another reason that Napoleon's novelistic narrative reached its end on St. Helena was that his famous inner fire went out. As the great warrior neared age fifty, his once boundless energy faded. He was headed toward death.

As you will find in chapter 15, some relatively recent devotees of Napoleon's story think that a villain hurried along the story's end. They have argued mightily—in books and articles—that someone, perhaps a prominent member of the emperor's own household, slowly poisoned Napoleon on St. Helena, robbing him of his ambition, his vigor, and ultimately his life. They argue that the 1821 autopsy finding—stating the cause of death as stomach cancer—was either the result of medical incompetence or an official cover-up for murder. Do they have a valid case? Was Napoleon poisoned? And if he was, how would anyone prove it almost two centuries later?

The mysteries like this one contained in these chapters are among history's greatest cold cases. Anthropologists, historians, amateur enthusiasts, medical researchers, and even modern detectives have sought to solve them. Investigators have used every means available—from the latest forensic technology to psychological analysis to educated guesses. In the absence of hard evidence, pure speculation sometimes casts new light on a long-ago motive.

These cold cases involve kings, queens, and their families—the best-known figures of their respective times. Several are the subjects of countless books and articles. According to historian John Clubbe, at least two hundred thousand books have been written about Napoleon alone. Yet there are questions about these famous lives—and in several cases, their mysterious deaths—the answers to which have eluded generations of biographers and investigators.

Did King Herod order a massacre of helpless children? Did Russia's Anastasia escape execution? What about the baffling 1567 murder of the Earl of Darnley, found strangled outside his blown-to-bits house? Did his wife, Mary Queen of Scots, have anything to do with that? The royal subjects range from ancient Egypt's Tutankhamen to modern Britain's Princess Diana, whose death in a 1997 automobile crash has inspired conspiracy theories ranging from the unsettling to the comical.

These investigative trails may have grown cold, but they can still lead us to fascinating discoveries. Even when investigators have uncovered a plausible answer to one of these questions, it usually raises even more questions—as in chapter 12. If a genetic disease really was the cause of King George III's famous descent into insanity, then why didn't other members of his family, afflicted with the same illness, also go mad? If you're a fan of historical sleuthing, the solutions that beget new mysteries are the most fun.

1

Who (or What) Killed King Tut?

When British archaeologist Howard Carter unsealed the tomb of Tutankhamen in 1922, he brought fame to the twelfth king of Egypt's eighteenth dynasty. King Tut, as we like to call him, enjoys recognition greater than that of any other Nile Valley monarch except perhaps Cleopatra. Carter also found a mystery in that tomb. It may even be a murder mystery—still unsolved, thirty-three hundred years after the young pharaoh's death. Some scientists see evidence that the embalmers had been hasty and careless, handling the body roughly. They also cite signs that workers furnished and decorated the tomb in a clumsy rush, as if somebody was trying to hide something. Then there are X-rays, taken in the 1960s and 1970s, showing hints of what may have been a violent death.

Tutankhamen reigned between 1333 and 1323 BCE, preceding Cleopatra and her Roman contemporaries by thirteen hundred years. To state the obvious, that's a very long time ago.

If it hadn't been for the unspoiled bounty of art and artifacts that Carter found with the young king's mummy, Tut might have remained lost to the ages. That appears to have been the idea. A slightly later pharaoh ordered that the names of Tut, his two immediate predecessors, and his immediate successor be erased from official records. Workers with chisels chipped the names from monuments and buildings, leaving blanks or substituting the hieroglyphs for the tyrant Horemheb, an army general who, for lack of a royal heir, ascended the throne in 1319 BCE. Horemheb backdated his reign by more than thirty years and reinvented himself as successor to Amenhotep III, Tutankhamen's grandfather. It was as if the royals who lived and ruled after the 1353 BCE death of Amenhotep the Magnificent and before Horemheb's takeover had never existed.

Why did Horemheb create this fiction? Why conduct a disinformation campaign, attempting to erase four pharaohs from history? His motive seems to have been rooted in the enigmatic character and the singularly strange reign of Tutankhamen's father, Akhenaton. Portrayed in ancient wall paintings and sculpture as the pharaoh with the elongated features—a jutting chin, a stretched-looking head, spidery fingers and toes—Akhenaton was a rebel who derailed fifteen-hundred-year-old religious values, political traditions, and military priorities. He left it to his survivors—including a bewildered, ten-year-old successor—to clean up the resultant mess.

Tutankhamen was not the boy's original name. He was born Tutankhaten, meaning "living image of the Aton." The name reflected Akhenaton's belief in a god of the sun disc, Aton, essentially a new deity that Akhenaton elevated above all the traditional Egyptian gods, replacing them. Tut was probably born in Akhetaton (now Amarna), a new capital city that the king ordered to be built in honor of the new god. The resemblance between the names Akhenaton and Akhetaton was not, of course, coincidental. The king's name meant "useful to Aton," the city's, "seat of Aton's power." Akhenaton had taken the throne as Amenhotep IV and then changed his name, just as he changed so many other things.

Not all Egyptologists agree that Tut was Akhenaton's son. The prince's origins—like those of several characters in this story—remain somewhat obscure. Some experts think that he and Smenkhkare, his immediate predecessor as pharaoh, were much younger brothers or half-brothers of Akhenaton, fellow sons of Amenhotep III. Both were also Akhenaton's sons-in-law, married to two of his daughters by his queen, Nefertiti. Royal practice was for royals to marry royals, sometimes even daughter to father, as a way to concentrate the purity of the bloodline. Smenkhkare and Tutankhamen were probably their wives' half-brothers, but they may instead have been their wives' uncles. Both widespread incest taboos and modern genetic science suggest that it's inadvisable for sisters, brothers, uncles, and nieces to conceive children with one another. Inbreeding narrows a gene pool, so that genetic defects become more likely to express themselves. The fate of Egypt's eighteenth dynasty may provide a cautionary tale on this subject. Some modern medical examiners of Tut's remains think that the kid may not have been quite right.

The boys (assuming that both of them were boys) likely were Akhenaton's but almost certainly were not born of the king's "great wife," Nefertiti. The great wife was the queen, but a king often had other, lesser wives. The burial place of Akhetaton shows evidence of a secondary wife, Kiya, who may have died giving birth to little Tut. At least, the timing seems right.

Smenkhkare remains an even more shadowy figure. One rather inventive line of thought says that he was not a brother or an uncle at all, but a woman, perhaps Nefertiti herself in the guise of a man. Whatever else the theory says, it illustrates that when evidence is lacking, imagination tends to take over, even among Egyptologists.

Why did Akhenaton change religions? Nobody knows, but it's reasonable to assume it was both a personal vision and an attempt to break free of the bureaucracy that had built up around his predecessors. A dense hierarchy of priests and scribes ran the government in Thebes. By tradition, the pharaoh himself was a god, the font of earthly authority. But ancient Egypt was a big nation with a rich history. It had been formed more than fifteen hundred years earlier by the union of two even more ancient societies. The theocracy over that time had spawned levels and levels of priestly administrators and their underling scribes. As in any hierarchy, there were politics—complex alliances and enmities of favor and privilege, ins and outs, bribery, and corruption.

It appears that Akhenaton did not like the games his people played. By turning his back on the old gods, including mighty Amon, king of the gods and patron of Thebes, Akhenaton undermined the priestly class.

Unlike Thebes, where temples had shadowy hallways and alcoves, the new capital featured roofless gardens of worship, open to the bright Egyptian sky. The style of royal art changed drastically. In subject matter, portrayals of idyllic domesticity replaced violent scenes of hunts and battles. Instead of being shown slaying foes or capturing slaves, the king is depicted at the dinner table, dandling his infant daughters, kissing his wife, and offering up libations to Aton. Unlike the traditional sun god, Re (or Ra), this new sun god was never depicted in human or animal form. Artists showed Re as a hawk-headed man with a snake—cobra or asp—encircling a sun disc balanced on top of his head. Aton, by contrast, was the disc unadorned, the sun itself.

Stylistically, the traditionally idealized form of the pharaoh was out. Artists, apparently by royal direction, instead showed the king's odd physiognomy—a long chin, narrow eyes, a slender neck somewhere between gracile and gawky, a weak-looking chest, and a pot belly exposed above a low-slung kilt that hugged wide hips and thick thighs.

If that's what Akhenaton really looked like, he may have had Marfan's syndrome, a disorder of the connective tissue that leads to unusual growth patterns. This genetic condition would account, especially, for the long head, the long chin, the narrow eyes, the pinched shoulders, and the long digits. Marfan's is expressed differently in different people, and the symptoms resemble those of some other disorders, so it is especially difficult to make a diagnosis from paintings or even photographs. Some scholars have suggested, but never proved, that U.S. president Abraham Lincoln's gangly build and unusual looks were evidence of Marfan's.

In the 1990s, Egyptologist Bob Brier talked to New Yorkers with Marfan's syndrome to gain insight into the pharaoh's character. Some of them told him that—especially in their youth—they flaunted the dramatic physical characteristics that made them look and feel so different from everyone else. Brier thinks Akhenaton, a rebellious sort, may have done that, too. Alternatively, he may simply have enjoyed expressionistic exaggerations in art.

As Akhenaton behaved like the head of an ancient flower-child cult, his country suffered a lack of leadership. Back in Thebes, the traditional priesthood struggled with loss of prestige and income. The city began to fall into disrepair. Tax revenues declined as the king neglected governmental oversight. Neighbor states decreased the amount of wealth sent to Egypt in tribute—money sent to keep the mighty superpower from invading. Egypt's ambassadors abroad sent dispatches pleading for military support, which did not come. Ambitious princes in places like Palestine and Assyria began to think that maybe Egypt wasn't so indomitable after all, and with good reason.

Akhenaton neither ventured into battle nor sent his army to enforce regional order. In fact, he declared that he would not step beyond the boundaries of his new city. The nation was in decline, in danger, and the king kept himself blissfully insulated.

A cheer must have gone up when Akhenaton died in 1336 BCE. His death presented a chance for restoration. Indeed, his successor Smenkhkare began to rehabilitate the cult of Amon. Smenkhkare's reign was short, however. He died young, succeeded by his little brother Tut, about nine or ten at the time. The boy's royal status and that of his progeny was cemented with his marriage to Akhenaton and Nefertiti's third-oldest daughter, Ankhesenpaaten, a few years older than he was.

During his minority, the new king was cared for by a regent, Ay, who occupied the office of prime minister. Despite having been Akhenaton's top priest to Aton, this political veteran was a realist. Bowing to pressure, Ay got to work on restoring the old, Thebes-based government. The young pharaoh's name was changed to Tutankhamen ("living image of Amon") and the teen queen's name became Ankhesenamen ("living through Amon"). The shift must have baffled and frightened the young couple, raised to worship their father's "one true god."

Little is known of Tut's life during his decade-long reign, except that like Smenkhkare before him, he died quite young, probably before he reached age twenty. Yet details about the way he was buried have raised suspicions that something unusual was going on around the time of his death.

For one thing, the tomb isn't right—not what a royal tomb should be. Because the contents are treasures of archaeology, priceless pieces of exquisite ancient art, people in the twenty-first century tend to think of Tut's tomb as an example of regal splendor. Yet that's entirely because it remained undiscovered and untampered with over thousands of years, while grave robbers took everything of value from the more stately tombs around it.

By comparison with other royal burial suites in the Valley of Kings area near Thebes, Tut's tomb is small to the point of unseemly. Many Egyptologists believe that Ay's larger tomb had originally been intended for Tut and that Tut's tomb had been built for the commoner Ay. Others think that Tut was buried in what was not a real tomb but essentially a storeroom, a place to put artifacts that had been rescued from the graves near Akheta-ton, which was becoming a ghost town.

Tombs contained possessions—spears, bows, arrows, bowls, wine jugs, chariots, and more—because ancient Egyptians be-lieved that a person would need them in the next world. Tut's cramped tomb was crammed with items, many quite beauti-ful, but few of them seemed to have belonged to him in life. Some bore the name of Smenkhkare. Many seemed haphaz-ardly shoved in, scattered as though placed with little care. The tomb opening was so narrow that axles had to be sawed in half so that chariots could be fit through the passage.

Tut's burial itself seems to have been botched. For one thing, the stone lid that covered his mummy doesn't match the rest of his sarcophagus. Instead, it is a damaged piece, apparently scav-enged from a different vessel and made of a different-colored stone. It was clumsily patched and painted to look as if it be-longed.

The mummy itself is a puzzle, too, although much of the fault for that lies with Carter and his 1920s colleagues. Archae-ologists of the time didn't understand the value of a mummy, what they might learn from it. They wanted to get at artifacts. The neckbands, the amulets, and the scarabs wrapped in the body covering interested them more than dried flesh did. Tut's body had been covered with embalming resin and fragrant oils, which had hardened over the many centuries, coating the funer-ary mask and cementing jewelry so that it could not, without great effort, be removed. Carter tried to soften this rock-hard layer by exposing the mummy to the hot Egyptian sun. When that didn't work, he and his assistants scraped and chipped at the hardened resin with hot knives. Still dissatisfied with their

progress, they resorted to cutting off the arms and the legs, sev-
ering the head, and even slicing the torso in two. Such mistreat-
ment caused rapid deterioration of the mummy, especially what
was left of the soft tissues.

Some experts think, however, that the body was damaged
much earlier, as it was being prepared for burial. For example, the king's breastbone is missing, and it appears that it may
have been so before embalmers wrapped the body. Egyptian embalmers customarily removed the brain and the major abdominal organs so that the corpse could be dried with natron salts (a
naturally occurring combination of sodium chloride, sodium car-
bonate, and sodium bicarbonate, harvested from dry lakebeds).
They did not, however, mess with the heart. Assumed to be the
seat of thinking, the heart was something the deceased would
need in the next world. There was not a custom of cracking the
chest.

The Egyptians didn't know what the brain was for, but they
knew that it was too moist to preserve well, so they—wait, perhaps this is a good place to warn the squeamish. If you don't
want to know what they did with the brain, skip the next para-
graph. Come to think of it, skip the next two paragraphs.

For those of you who don't mind this sort of thing, the Egyptian embalmers needed to get the soggy old brain out of the skull
without spoiling the deceased's good looks. Their method was to
take out the gray matter through the nose, but very few people
have brains small enough to fit through their noses. The embalmers got around this difficulty by liquefying the gray matter.
They stuck a long, thin tool up one nostril, breaking through
the sinus bone and into the cranial cavity. Then they whipped
their tool around like a whisk until the brain was the con-
sistency of raw egg. Turning the corpse over onto its stomach,
the embalmers then drained the liquid out the nose. Next, they
turned the body over again and poured in hot resin to cauterize
any remaining tissue and coat the inside of the skull with this
preservative.

Other organs came out through a neat slit cut into the left side of the abdomen. The embalmer reached in, felt around blindly with one hand, and cut out the organs one by one with a knife held in the other hand. In Tut's case, the incision appears ragged and too long—sloppy work, say latter-day critics.

None of this would necessarily have raised suspicions of foul play if it were not for X-ray images of the mummy, taken in 1968 by scientists from the University of Liverpool, and another set shot ten years later by a University of Michigan research team. The images revealed what appears to be a bone chip inside the head. Was this caused by pre-death trauma to the skull? It took years, but scientists finally agreed that it was not. If the bone chip had been there at the time of embalming, it would have been glued to the inside of the skull by the resin. Buried in hardened resin, which appears opaque on X-rays, the chip would not have shown up so clearly on the images. Still, the subject of violent death had been raised.

The head also seemed to have suffered what might have been a blow or even a puncture at the lower back left, just behind the ear. Some radiologists saw a shadow that they thought indicated a subdural hematoma, an injury caused by trauma such as a sharp blow to the head or in some cases by a tumor or a burst aneurysm. Internal bleeding can lead to a calcium deposit that would show up on an X-ray, even thousands of years later, as a thickening of the bone. Some radiologists thought, however, that this was an illusion caused by the way the resin had settled before it hardened. Tut also appeared to have suffered an abrasion to one cheek and a broken leg—although examiners weren't sure whether the bone was broken before or after he died.

Another suspicious oddity occurs in a bit of wall art within the tomb. It shows the priest performing the traditional opening of the mouth ceremony—a symbolic preparation for Tut's next life. Writing on the wall clearly identifies the priest as Ay, the prime minister. Yet he is wearing a pharaoh's headdress. In fact, the aged Ay succeeded Tut as pharaoh. But the new king traditionally took the crown after the old one was laid to rest, not before. What was going on?

In 2002 Michael R. King and Gregory R. Cooper, veteran police investigators from Utah, tried to apply modern crime detection procedures to Tut's death. With the help of archaeological, historical, and medical experts, they developed a case that pointed to Ay as a possible murderer. At nineteen, Tut was well into adulthood by his society's standards. Was he ruling on his own, making decisions that prime minister Ay did not approve of? Had Tut shown signs of bucking the system, as his father had done? Could Ay have committed murder, or ordered murder, to keep history from repeating itself?

Ay certainly had access to the victim, and as the government's most powerful minister, he had means to cover up his crime. He may have used his authority to rush the funeral and his own coronation so that the transfer of power would be complete before the country's top general, Horemheb, returned from a military campaign.

Tut left no heirs. His wife, Ankhesenamen, had miscarried twice, a detail known because the young couple had taken the unusual step of mummifying the stillborns, both girls and both exhibiting signs of spine deformities. One of them seems to have had spina bifida, a congenital rift of the backbone.

Because Ay was not royal by birth, he needed a way to legitimize his rule. Most experts believe that he married the widowed young queen for this purpose. Antiquarians cite the existence of two ceramic rings dated to the period and linking the names of Ay and Ankhesenamen—probably two surviving examples of party favors from a wedding feast. There is some evidence that Ay had other marriage ties to the royals. Amenhotep III had taken the unusual step of marrying a commoner, and Ay may have been the brother of that queen, Tiy. Historian Paul Doherty thinks it likely that Ay was also the father of Nefertiti.

If so, then Ankhesenamen may have been his granddaughter before she became his wife.

Even so, she was a queen by birth and he, her social inferior. The most intriguing bit of evidence that something was rotten in Thebes is a document discovered far to the north, in Turkey. Among the records of the ancient Hittite civilization, there is an account of letters written by an Egyptian queen to the Hittite king Suppiluliuma. The letters stated that her husband was dead, that she had no son, that she was afraid, and that she refused to take her servant as husband. She pleaded with the Hittite king to send one of his sons to her, promising to marry the prince and make him pharaoh. That queen was almost certainly Ankhesenamen.

The Hittites and the Egyptians were enemies, so Suppiluliuma cautiously investigated before sending a son to Egypt. He must have confirmed that the invitation was genuine. Yet someone intercepted that young Hittite and his entourage and took care to kill him before he reached Egypt. Did Ay send a patrol to murder the foreign prince? Was Ay the "servant" whom the queen refused to marry? Michael King, Gregory Cooper, Brier, and other investigators think it likely. They also raise the possibility that Ay and General Horemheb were co-conspirators, and that Horemheb did the killing.

Ay was nearly sixty, quite old by standards of the time, when he became pharaoh. He ruled less than four years and then died. At that point, Horemheb suppressed Ay's chosen successor and took the throne for himself. How did Horemheb claim royal legitimacy? Perhaps he felt that after the precedent of Ay, the first commoner-pharaoh, he didn't need legitimacy, that his control of the army sufficed. Or perhaps Ankhesenamen wrote to the Hittite king a few years later than is commonly thought. Perhaps she was afraid of Horemheb, not of Ay. Perhaps it was the general who was forcing her to marry him. Maybe her alliance with Grandpa Ay had not been matrimonial but purely political.

At any rate, Horemheb was the pharaoh who erased the names of Akhenaton, Smenkhkare, Tutankhamen, and Ay from Egyptian history, backdating his own reign. He also abolished the cult of Aton. Obviously, he must have harbored antipathy toward Tut, if only for the boy's origins. Could he have been the murderer?

What if Tutankhamen wasn't killed? Doherty engaged a radiologist to take a fresh look at the old X-rays of the mummy. His expert interpreted the condition of the spine as evidence of fused vertebra—perhaps from a congenital defect passed along to the king's stillborn daughters. The historian notes that Tut is often depicted in surviving art as either leaning on a walking stick or sitting. In one wall painting, he shoots his bow from a seated position while Queen Ankhesenamen, crouched at his feet, passes him another arrow. There were more than forty walking sticks among the artifacts in his tomb.

Doherty theorizes that Tutankhamen had been disabled from birth. Other paintings that show him driving a chariot and making war may have been part of a campaign to make him appear far healthier than he was. If the boy inherited Marfan's syndrome from his father, the disorder may have expressed itself in spinal problems and also in a deformed sternum that jutted out, a condition called "pigeon chest." Such a breastbone, ill-formed and fragile, might have easily been crushed during the embalming process. Doherty notes that another mummy, probably that of Smenkhkare because of its close physical resemblance to Tut's, also is missing the breastbone. Perhaps they shared an affliction. And perhaps that affliction, which can increase the likelihood of an aneurism, killed Tutankhamen.

In 2005, a team of Egyptian scientists led by Zahi Hawass, the nation's most distinguished authority on antiquities, made new images of King Tut's mummy, this time using CT scan technology. Their interpretation of the pictures is that the king was neither a murder victim nor disabled. Although he had an elongated skull—like his father's in the paintings—the trait was not outside the range of normal head shape, said the scientists. An unnatural bend in the spine, they ruled, probably happened after death, during embalming.

Hawass announced that most members of the team, although not all of them, thought the king had died of gangrene, the result of a compound fracture of his leg. They speculate that the infected wound had killed him rather quickly. They saw no evidence of a blow to the head. It should be noted that CT scans, like X-rays, require interpretation. Even using twenty-first-century technology, radiologists can disagree about the nature or the origin of a shadowy mass within a brain or a bone. Other experts will examine the seventeen hundred images that the Egyptian researchers shot, and some of them may disagree with the Hawass team's conclusion.

Until then, it seems most reasonable to accept the recent finding—that King Tut's death was an accident. Maybe Tutankhamen was a reckless driver who crashed his chariot. Then again, maybe an assassin sabotaged the chariot or deliberately frightened his horses.

To investigate further:

Brier, Bob. *The Murder of Tutankhamen: A True Story.* New York: G. P. Putnam's Sons, 1971. The Egyptologist and TV host tells a story of political intrigue that could have led to the young king's death.

Carter, Howard, and A. C. Mace. *The Discovery of the Tomb of Tutankhamen* (new edition). New York: Dover Publications, 1977. First-hand account of the discovery.

Doherty, Paul. *The Mysterious Death of Tutankhamun.* New York: Caroll & Graf, 2002. A historical novelist reconstructs events surrounding the king's death to read like a thriller.

El Mahdy, Christine. *Tutankhamen: The Life and Death of the Boy-King.* New York: St. Martin's Press, 1999. An Egyptologist overturns historical misconceptions by highlighting details of the king's reign and life.

King, Michael R., and Gregory M. Cooper. *Who Killed King Tut? Using Modern Forensics to Solve a 3,300-Year-Old Mystery*. Amherst, NY: Prometheus Books, 2004. Trained as police detectives, the authors tackle the ultimate cold case.

Netzley, Patricia D. *The Curse of King Tut*. San Diego, CA: Lucent Books, 2000. A brief and accessible summary of the king's life and death.

Reeves, Nicholas. *The Complete Tutankhamun: The King, the Tomb, the Royal Treasure*. New York: Thames and Hudson, 1995. An illustrated guide to treasures of the tomb.

2

Did King Herod Slaughter Bethlehem's Babies?

B lame it on the magi. In the Gospel According to Matthew, these stargazing travelers showed up at the Jerusalem palace of Herod I, the king of Judea, to ask directions. Also known as the three wise men or the three kings (of Orient), they'd come to find "he that is born king of the Jews."

A "star of wonder, star of light," as the Christmas carol describes it, had tipped them off about the baby and led them from a land or lands in the east—India, Persia, and Arabia have been suggested—to Judea and to Herod. If the magi were indeed kings, or even minor nobles, they did the right thing when they checked in with the local ruler. Diplomatic etiquette would have demanded as much. Besides, they apparently needed a bit of help finding what they were looking for. Stars are great for large-scale navigation across oceans and deserts, but they are less useful when it comes to steering you to a specific street address.

Herod was no help. When the travelers asked him where they could find this king, a strange look appeared on Herod's face. As far as he knew, there was only one king of the Jews and he was it. The Roman Senate had bestowed that title upon him in 40 BCE, and he'd had to fight to make it a reality. Over the decades since, he had gone to considerable lengths to protect the trademark. Any kid trying on the title for size didn't know with whom he was messing.

Herod told the magi to go search out this "king" and when they found him to come right back to the palace with a report. They went, finding the baby a little south of Jerusalem in a town called Bethlehem (now in the Palestinian West Bank). Impressed with the child, whose name was Jesus, they bowed down before him and gave him the presents they had lugged across the desert: gold and really expensive aromatic resins. What they did not do is go back and tell Herod where to find the boy. A dream warned one or more of the magi that great harm would befall Jesus if they did what Herod had ordered. So they took an alternate route and slipped quietly out of Judea.

Herod wanted to preempt any attempt, however unlikely it must have seemed, to take away his crown and give it to a toddler. After the magi stood him up, the angry king decided to play it safe. If he couldn't find and murder the specific little boy who threatened him, he would simply kill all the infants of about the right age, in Bethlehem and the surrounding districts.

Herod carried out his horrific plan, but it didn't work. He killed a lot of babies, but Jesus wasn't among them. That's because an angel told Joseph, the baby's (earthly) dad, to take his family south into Egypt until it was safe to come back.

The slaughter of the innocents, as this episode is called, presents a problem for historians. No one, except the apostle Matthew, seems to have noted it. This is odd, because Herod's life and reign were well-known. He associated with Cassius (the assassin of Julius Caesar), Mark Antony (the avenger of Julius

Caesar), and Augustus Caesar (who defeated Antony to become Rome's first emperor). These Roman leaders fought one another, but each in turn relied on Herod to take care of Roman Judea. This fact puts Herod in rather well-documented historical company.

Appointed by his father, who also worked for the Romans, Herod became governor of Galilee (the northern portion of ancient Palestine) in 47 BCE. Four years later, upon the assassination of his father, he became governor of Judea, centered on Jerusalem. Later yet, he had to defeat a contender to establish himself as king (still propped up by the Romans), and he held on to that job with cunning, efficiency, and brutality for more than thirty years. Much of what Herod did, including building the great temple at Jerusalem, has been passed down in writing. Yet the source for the story of the slaughter is a very few verses in a single book of the New Testament. The other Gospel accounts—the books of Mark, Luke, and John—make no mention of the slaughter. And it shows up only in passing in a historical account.

Why don't other sources recount this outrage? Wouldn't something that horribly cruel have been the talk of the Middle East? It certainly caught the attention of religious artists in the Renaissance. They painted lurid scenes of soldiers pulling screaming babes from the arms of desperate, clinging mothers. (Another favorite theme of later religious art was the beheading of John the Baptist by Herod I's son and heir, Herod Antipas.)

Did King Herod cover up the massacre? How could he pull it off? The answer may lie in the magnitude of the alleged crime and its context within this king's bloody rule.

Born in 73 BCE, Herod was a Jew, but he was of Edomite Arab heritage. That made him something of an outsider in Judea, but it was actually an advantage in gaining and keeping power. Herod, like his father before him, ruled not by hereditary right or by popularity among the governed; the governed hated him.

He did it by kissing up to a superpower—Rome. The Romans liked to back leaders who depended on Rome, not on their own people, for support. It gave the Romans leverage.

Herod's father, Antipater, had been a courtier to the Hasmonean kings, the longtime dynastic rulers of Judea. After a family dispute among the royals opened the door to Roman takeover, Julius Caesar allowed a Hasmonean heir to continue in the post of high priest but stripped him of administrative power, giving that instead to Antipater.

Residents of Judea resented the change in rule and the dominance by Rome. Herod, whose fortunes rose with his father's, showed no sympathy. As governor of Galilee, he chased down a rebel group whose members refused to pay their taxes. Hunting them with ruthless, Roman-style efficiency, he slaughtered many. Then he tortured and killed the group's leader, Ezekias, who had been something of a folk hero to many Jews. Called before the Great Sanhedrin, the traditional Jewish judicial council, to answer for his brutality, Herod made a defiant show, confident that his Roman overlords would protect him. He was correct.

After his father's assassination (by poisoned wine), Herod stepped up to the post of governor, serving alongside the Hasmonean high priest Hyrcanus, whom Herod defended against rebel armies. In gratitude, Hyrcanus gave Herod his daughter Mariamme as a wife.

Herod defended Hyrcanus from homegrown rebellion, but he wasn't able to protect the priest from Antigonus, also a Hasmonean heir and Hyrcanus's brother. Antigonus attacked Judea with a force of Parthians, from Persia. Herod fled to Rome and got himself declared king by the Senate, and then returned with a force of mercenaries—Romans, Arabs, Greeks, and even Germanic tribesmen from the north (but few, if any, Jews). Although Antigonus lost the war for control of Judea, he took Hyrcanus prisoner. Some accounts of this story say that Antigonus ordered that his brother's ears be cut off. Other versions say that Antigonus personally bit off the priest's ears. Then he sold Hyrcanus to the Parthians. This was not an era of peace and goodwill, even between brothers.

Always one to hold a grudge, Herod, the new king, remembered the judges of the Sanhedrin, who had tried to discipline him for his brutality in putting down the earlier Galilee rebellion. He ordered forty-five of the seventy-one judges killed, replacing them with his own cronies.

Herod had at least ten wives, two of them named Mariamme. Of those, the first Mariamme, the daughter of Hyrcanus, occupied a special place in his story, because he actually seemed to love her. At least, he was jealous of her affections. She was also special because he killed her—although that was after he thought she was plotting to kill him. First, however, he killed her eighteen-year-old brother, Aristobulus.

Although still a teen, Aristobulus was a genuine Hasmonean prince. With Hyrcanus gone, Herod needed to appoint a new high priest. Mariamme lobbied hard for her little brother to get the post. Herod finally agreed, thinking the move might smooth things over with the traditionalists.

The Judeans loved Aristobulus. They loved him so much that Herod began to worry. What if supporters rose up and tried to make Aristobulus the king? To eliminate that possibility, Herod invited his young brother-in-law to a pool party. Aristobulus joined in the fun, splashing and playing dunking games. The games ended when everybody realized that Aristobulus had been underwater a little too long. He was dead.

Herod's mother-in-law, Alexandra, did not buy the story about an accidental drowning. She'd never liked Herod in the first place. She tried to enlist the help of Cleopatra, the queen of Egypt (and at the time keeping house with Mark Antony of Rome), in a plot against Herod. At Cleopatra's urging, Antony sent for Herod. Facing the possibility that Antony might sentence him to death for the murder of Aristobulus, Herod couldn't stand the thought of the beautiful Mariamme, his widow, with another man. He would rather see her dead, and he left instructions to that effect.

Herod's uncle Joseph, who was supposed to carry out the death sentence, let the secret slip to Mariamme. She was not touched by her husband's devotion. She convinced Joseph to help her escape, if necessary. Herod, acquitted of the murder charge, came home to a palace full of accusations. His mother and his sister told him that Mariamme had planned to run away. His sister threw in the charge that Mariamme had been having an affair with Joseph. At first, Herod didn't believe it, but later he decided that the only way Mariamme could have learned about the order to kill her was by sleeping with his uncle. Joe got the death sentence, but Mariamme got another chance.

Leaving for a later trip, however, the king gave another care-taker the same order: in the event of Herod's death, kill Mari-amme. Mariamme a persuasive woman, found out again. When Herod got back, Mariamme was angry and refused to sleep with him, but he didn't know why. Herod's sister convinced him that his wife was plotting to kill him. To learn more, Herod tortured Mariamme's favorite servant. He learned that Mariamme had charmed the truth about his death order out of another care-taker. So the king killed that caretaker. Then he put Mariamme on trial for treason and sentenced her to death.

Herod fell ill, supposedly with grief and remorse, after he killed Mariamme in 29 BCE. Alexandra saw his illness as an op-portunity. She tried to raise a revolt against him, but he recov-ered enough to catch on. He had her killed as well.

Among the several children whom Mariamme had borne Herod were two sons, Alexander and Aristobulus (the second apparently named after his murdered uncle). As Herod did with other of his children, he had sent them to Rome as youngsters so that they could learn how to govern in the Roman style. The other reason for this arrangement was so that the Romans would have another bit of collateral to ensure Herod's loyalty.

By virtue of their mother's heritage, Alexander and Aristobulus were Hasmonean princes. They were also very angry young men when they returned to Judea and found out what their father had done to Mariamme. They began to gather support for a Hasmonean coup against Herod. Once again, however, the plotters failed to keep a secret from Herod's spies. Herod arrested his sons and put them on trial before Augustus Caesar himself, but the emperor dismissed the charges.

Frustrated, Herod called on another son, Antipater, whose mother was Herod's first wife, intending to make him sole heir. Antipater didn't like Dad any more than his half-brothers did, and he decided he'd rather ascend to the throne sooner instead of later. He began to plot against the king on his own, while Alexander and Aristobulus tried to come up with a method to knock off both Herod and Antipater.

Herod arrested his two sons by Mariamme once again and appealed to Augustus Caesar a second time. This time, the emperor gave special permission for the king of Judea to kill his sons. Herod found them guilty of treason and ordered them strangled to death.

The people of Judea had never liked Herod, although they marveled at his architectural feats and were deeply grateful for the grand temple that he built to replace the earlier temples that had stood on Temple Mount. (Jerusalem's famous Wailing Wall is all that remains of Herod's temple.) The king is known as Herod the Great both in honor of his achievements, largely as a builder and an administrator, and to distinguish him from successors who were also named Herod.

The Judeans appreciated Herod's efficiency and recognized a strain of compassion that somehow accompanied his brutality. When a crop failure threatened Judea with mass starvation, the king dipped into his own coffers to buy grain from Egypt and have it milled and baked into bread. He used soldiers to distribute the bread so that it reached those who needed it. He also appealed to the Romans on behalf of the Jews, as when he won them immunity from service in Rome's army. Finally, he was known to extend tax relief.

Still, he earned such a reputation for ruthless cruelty that he was the farthest thing from a beloved ruler. By itself, his complicity with Rome would have made him unpopular, no matter how good he'd been at governance. The people of Judea, especially those who took their heritage and religion most seriously, never became comfortable with Roman domination. They blamed Herod for killing off the Hasmonean heirs, still seen as legitimate rulers. Besieged by plots, Herod became even more suspicious and spiteful and even more intolerant of any challenge to his authority.

Late in his reign, the aged Herod ordered a golden eagle insignia, the symbol of imperial Rome, affixed above the main entrance of the great temple. Many Jews took offense. How could they tolerate the symbol of the foreign oppressor over the door of their holy place?

In an act of protest, a group of Torah students, led by Pharisee rabbis, cut down the eagle. Herod—increasingly frail, weak, and ever more paranoid—had them arrested and burned alive, then proceeded to have other religious rebels burned, too. Not long before Herod died—probably in 4 BCE—he ordered that Antipater, still plotting against the old man, be poisoned.

The magi story in Matthew is sketchy. For example, the apostle doesn't even say how many of them came in search of Jesus. The tradition that there were three, and that their names were Kaspar, Balthasar, and Melchior, came about later in the Roman Catholic Church. In the Eastern Orthodox version of the story, there are not three wise men but twelve.

If there were magi following a star (or simply traveling west on business) and if indeed they visited Herod, they would have been met by the late version of the king—the tyrant at his worst. More than five hundred years after this, a Christian scholar named Dionysius Exiguus calculated the year of Jesus' birth and used it to create a calendar; it is the basis of the calendar we still use today. Dionysius's calendar started with the nativity, so people still think of Jesus as being born in the year 1 CE (or AD). Later scholars, measuring the events in the Gospels against other historical sources and astronomic calculations, realized that Dionysius's math was off by four to seven years. That is, Jesus was born sometime between 7 and 4 BCE. Thus, when this religious figure was a baby in Bethlehem, Herod was a bitter, friendless old monarch, insane with distrust and paranoia, and probably wracked with guilt over his murders of those closest to him. This was the Herod who ordered his own boys strangled and poisoned, the Herod who allegedly enjoyed watching and listening to the religious protesters he had condemned as they writhed and screamed in the agonies of death by fire. At the end, he changed his will over and over again, paralyzed by suspicions against the sons (by other wives) who remained to succeed him.

This Herod, if he thought there was even a hint of threat in a baby "king of the Jews," would certainly have ordered the child killed. It is entirely in keeping with his character that he would murder other children, perhaps many children.

But why wouldn't such a crime be reported, committed to some public record that would have survived into history? Perhaps the reason for this is that the massacre—as horrific as it was—didn't qualify as that big a deal. Modern Bethlehem is a city of about forty thousand, but ancient Bethlehem was quite a small town by most accounts. How small is a matter of some dispute. Matthew says that Herod "sent forth and slew all the children that were in Bethlehem, and in all the coasts thereof, from two years old and under." What were "the coasts thereof"? In the original Greek text, the word has a meaning more akin to "districts." Does that mean in all the parts of Bethlehem? Does it mean also in the surrounding countryside? How many children under age two were there in and around Bethlehem at the time? Fewer than twenty? More than two hundred? If widespread slaughter was common, and under Herod's rule that appears to have been the case, the deaths of hundreds of children would probably still raise an outcry. What if, however, the numbers killed were more in the range of a few dozen children? Would that make the history books?

Another factor would be the income and the social status of the families whose children were targeted. Impoverished families may have had no one to whom they could appeal, especially as Herod had gutted the traditional Jewish justice system.

Skeptics point out that the story of a king or a noble who fears a child and tries (usually failing) to have that child killed crops up throughout ancient texts. In Hindu scripture, the wicked king of Mathura, learning from a prophecy that his sister's son will slay him, arranges for all her children to be killed but misses Krishna, who has been smuggled across the river to safety. Krishna survives to grow into the greatest of the gods. In Greek mythology an oracle warns the king of Thebes to fear his unborn son. After the baby arrives, the king tries to abandon the boy, but a kindly shepherd rescues him. That child grows up to be Oedipus. These and other stories bear a resemblance to the slaughter of the innocents and the holy family's flight into Egypt. So, yes, the slaughter of the innocents could be a myth in the same vein, but a lot of stories—some true, some fantastic—contain parallel plotlines. It could also be noted that Herod's domestic life—sons against fathers, in-laws against in-laws, adultery, and murder—resembles an incredibly lurid soap opera plot, yet it really happened.

Herod's rise and reign were chronicled in the greatest detail by the historian Josephus (also known as Flavius Josephus), in a work titled *Antiquities of the Jews*. Published almost a century after Herod's death, it does make a brief reference to the massacre of the innocents, although Josephus seems to mix up the murder of Herod's adult sons with the murders of the infants. He also places the incident in Syria, not in Judea.

If Josephus had gotten the tale directly from the Book of Matthew (probably first written down around 70 CE), the historian's details probably would have matched those of the apostle. That they don't suggests that Josephus relied on a separate written source or an oral tradition telling of Herod's slaughter of the children. In other words, the tale was known. That doesn't make it true, of course.

It may never be proved that the slaughter of the innocents took place. Yet it also seems impossible to disprove it. Herod was certainly capable of horrible cruelty, especially when he perceived any threat to his authority. Late in life, when the massacre supposedly took place, he was also off his rocker. Given who and what Herod was, the story could have been invented and widely believed because it sounded just like something the old psychopath would do. Whether he did or didn't slaughter Bethlehem's babies, the king of Judea was certainly a murderer many times over.

To investigate further:

Aune, David E. *The Gospel of Matthew in Current Study: Studies in Memory of William G. Thompson, S.J.* Grand Rapids, MI: Wm. B. Eerdmans Publishing, 2001. An examination of the biblical source of the slaughter story.

Geoghegan, Jeffrey C., and Michael M. Homan. *The Bible for Dummies*. Hoboken, NJ: John Wiley & Sons, 2002. An easy-to-use guide for anybody and everybody.

Grant, Michael. *Herod the Great*. New York: American Heritage, 1971. A detailed biography from historical sources.

Green, Robert. *Herod the Great*. New York: Franklin Watts, 1996. A basic introduction for young people.

Perowne, Stewart. *The Life and Times of Herod the Great*. Stroud, Glouster-shire, UK: Sutton, 2003. The author paints a somewhat sympathetic portrait of Herod.

Richardson, Peter. *Herod: King of the Jews and Friend of the Romans*. Columbia: University of South Carolina Press, 1996. A scholarly account that focuses sharply on the king's character.

Sandmel, Samuel. *Herod: Profile of a Tyrant*. Philadelphia: J. B. Lippencott, 1967. The author, a biblical scholar, uses scriptural interpretation to explore Herod's life and reign.

3

Who Was the Real King Arthur?

Long before the Monty Python troupe and Walt Disney got hold of the legend, almost a millennium before Sir Thomas Malory immortalized the tale in the fifteenth century, the storytellers of Wales talked of the warrior Arthur. He led the allied kings of the Britons into battle, turning away Saxon invaders and preserving a way of life. Was there ever really such a king? Did his knights encircle a round table in Camelot? Was he trained by a canny wizard, and did he wield a magic sword pulled from a stone?

The wizardly bits of magic are obviously inventions—elements of mythical lore and superstition that crept, perhaps through gradual exaggeration, into folktales and romances about King Arthur. But what about Arthur himself? Did he really rule, fight, and love? Was he betrayed and slain by the evil Mordred? Did he live at all?

The short answer is no. The Arthur of T. H. White's 1958 book *The Sword in the Stone* (and the 1963 animated movie based on it) never lived. There was no king like the one depicted in the 1960 stage musical *Camelot* (based on White's *The Once and Future King*) and its 1967 film version. The hero of Sir Thomas Malory's *Le Morte d'Arthur* is an indisputably fictional character. Yet these and countless other literary incarnations of the king—ranging from the godlike to the idiotic (in Monty Python's spoof *Monty Python and the Holy Grail*)—stem from a tradition that could have started with something real, perhaps a real man.

Archaeological evidence indicates that the Christian Britons of Wales and what are now the English counties of Shropshire, Somerset, Devon, and Cornwall—then a scattering of small Celtic kingdoms—experienced a kind of renaissance around the year 500, well after the end of Roman Britannia. Signs of resurgence in building and trade may be evidence that a strong leader had brought about a period of peace—relief from the constant incursions of pagan Saxons from the east, and perhaps even a temporary respite from the warring that so often pitted these mini-kingdoms against one another.

Could this peace have come about thanks to a great leader called Arthur? The name suddenly became popular in the sixth century, as though Britons were naming their male children after a recent hero. If this is true, who was he?

Generations of modern investigators—literary scholars, historians, and archaeologists—have attempted to solve that mystery. None has been entirely successful in matching the legendary Arthur to a specific flesh-and-blood individual. The problem is that virtually nothing in the way of contemporary writings survives from the period when Arthur most likely lived.

Between 43 CE and about 410, most of the island of Britain—the lands that would later be England and Wales—was part of the Roman Empire. Rome brought a certain political stability to the island, along with the Christian faith (which seems to have taken hold in the third century). Roman troops kept clans and tribes of Britons from warring with one another. Just as important, the legions stood against potential invaders—Picts from the north, Irish from the west, Germanic tribes from what would later be Denmark and the Jutland region of Germany.

Then in 407, during one of the empire's periodic power struggles, a Roman soldier serving in Britain declared himself Emperor of the West (the western part of the vast empire). To establish his claim, he pulled Roman troops from Britain to fight rivals on the European continent. The legions did not return. Britons, long used to life under Roman protection, were suddenly vulnerable—to attackers from over the water and also to factionalism that pitted clan against clan, region against region. This was the beginning of the island's Dark Ages. Scholars place Arthur, if there was an Arthur, within this time.

Investigators have not lacked for candidates. Scarce scraps of history suggest an array of Roman-British commanders, as well as leaders of the British warlord royalty, who tried to fill the power vacuum after Rome's withdrawal.

Among the Romans, the centurion Lucius Artorius Castus seems—at least to some experts—a likely Arthur. He commanded troops guarding Hadrian's Wall—a barrier that protected Roman Britannia against the Picts, a warrior people living in what later became Scotland. His name alone, Artorius, puts him in the running, as proposed by the American medievalist Kemp Malone. Other scholars have suggested that Artorius commanded a contingent of Sarmatians, soldiers from a region that would later be southern Ukraine and the eastern Balkans. Among Sarmatian folktales are stories of a king with parallels to Arthur, including his dying command that his magic sword be flung into a lake—just as in the Arthurian legends Excalibur must be returned to the goddesslike Lady of the Lake. Could the conflation of Artorius and Sarmatian storytelling have become an early part of the Arthurian legend?

The 2004 movie *King Arthur* depicts Artorius (played by Clive Owen) as Arthur and makes the warrior princess Guinevere (played by Kiera Knightly) the daughter of Merlin (a Woadish king, whatever "Woadish" means). A 2004 video game, also called *King Arthur*, is based on the film. So Artorius has supporters in twenty-first-century pop culture, that most discriminating arena for historical ideas.

Yet at the core of the Arthurian legend are the king's battles against Saxons (a name also applied to Angles and Jutes, all of whom established their own post-Roman kingdoms in eastern Britain and became, considerably later, the English). A work called *Historia Brittonum*, written sometime after 820, tells of Saxons from Kent attacking the Britons and of Arthur riding with the British kings against them. Flourishing in the second century, Artorius did not fight Saxons. If Artorius was the inspiration for Arthur, his name must somehow have been attached erroneously to the Battle of Mt. Badon (*Mons Badonicus* in Latin), when Arthur and the Britons prevailed. Scholars place this crucial battle in the late fifth or early sixth century, hundreds of years after the Roman's death.

Another possible Arthur is Riothamus, a military commander of the fifth century, who, in about 470, led a force of "Brittones" against Visigoth invaders in Gaul (what is now France). His claim rests in part on another historical work, *The Origin of the Deeds of the Gauls*, published in 551. The author, a churchman called Jordanes, refers to Riothamus as "king of the Brittones."

The historian Geoffrey Ashe, an Arthur authority, has pointed out parallels between Riothamus's life and the legend of Arthur. Among them, Riothamus's lieutenant betrayed Riothamus much as Arthur is said to have been betrayed by his nephew Medraut (in later versions of the story, by his illegitimate son, Mordred). Also, when last heard of, after a defeat at the hands of the Visigoths, Riothamus was near a town called Avallon, in central France. The writer Geoffrey of Monmouth, a twelfth-century Welsh popularizer of the Arthur stories, wrote that the mortally wounded Arthur was carried off to the island of Avallon (later spelled Avalon) and not heard of again. Advocates of this theory also say that Riothamus was a title meaning something like "most royal" and that the man's baptismal name appears to have been Artorius.

Critics counter by pointing out that Riothamus led his "Brittones" under the banner of the Roman emperor Anthemius. If Riothamus was a high king from the island of Britain, why would he respond to Anthemius's call? Rome had pulled its troops out of Britain decades earlier, leaving the residents to defend themselves. The Britons owed no further allegiance to Rome.

Is it possible that Jordanes was referring to the people who came to be known as Bretons? After Rome abandoned Britain, many natives migrated south from Cornwall, across the English Channel to a peninsula that came to be named after them, the region of France still known as Brittany. Could Riothamus have been the Roman administrator or the Roman client-king of Brittany? If he was, would it disqualify him as the Arthur beloved of the Welsh and the English?

The biggest problem in identifying Riothamus as Arthur is the date at which he disappeared—around 470. That would seem a bit too early for the Battle of Camlan (or Camlann), named by Geoffrey of Monmouth as Arthur's final fight. Reliable dates, however, are exceedingly difficult to find among the evidence in this mystery. A tenth-century chronicle, *Annales Cambriae*, sets the Battle of Mt. Badon, when Arthur and the united British kings defeated the Saxons, in 516. It sets the Battle of Camlann, when Arthur and Medraut were slain—perhaps in

a royal family power struggle—in 537. Gildas the Wise, a Celtic
Christian monk born around 494, wrote that the Battle of Mt.
Badon took place in the year of his birth.

As a near contemporary, Gildas is probably more correct
than Geoffrey is. Most scholars place the Battle of Mt. Badon
within a decade of the year 500, more or less. Also, Mt. Badon
has always been described as somewhere within Britain. Some
think the battle happened near Bath (perhaps once called
Bathon) or near Cadbury Castle, an Iron Age hill fort in Dorset.
Instead of disappearing in Gaul, did the wounded Riothamus
recover and travel west across the Channel to fight Saxons?

Scotland also has its would-be Arthurs, including at least
one with the right name, Artuir mac Áedáin, a war leader of the
Scotti (forebears of the Scots) in the frontier region between
what had formerly been Roman-ruled Britannia and the northern wilds where Pictish tribes lived. Artuir led a confederation
of Christian Celts against the pagan northerners in a hundred-
mile-wide strip of Britain bounded by Hadrian's Wall to the
south and the Antonine Wall, another Roman fortification, to
the north.

As with virtually every proposed Arthur, there are problems
with this Scot's curriculum vitae. Picts were fierce pagans, like
the Saxons of this time, but they were otherwise quite unlike
the Germanic invaders specified in the Arthurian legends. Also,
Artuir appears to have flourished decades later than any date
proposed for the Battle of Camlann, when Arthur fell. Rather
than being the original Arthur, he may have been part of the
first wave of British babies named for the legend. The parallels
between his life and the legend may have been intentional. That
is, Artuir may have conducted himself after the manner of the
legendary Arthur and may even have directed that his burial
follow an Arthurian theme.

Back in Wales and the west midlands of England, Ambrosius Arelianus, another king of the post-Roman Britons, is our

next contestant. Gildas wrote of him as a survivor of a Saxon massacre, who calmly channeled his sorrow and rage into organizing the Britons into an opposing force and driving back the heathens. Geoffrey of Monmouth later also named Ambrosius as a king of the Britons who fought the Saxons, but in Geoffrey's telling, Ambrosius had a younger brother, Uther Pendragon—the father of Arthur.

Who was Uther? The writers Graham Phillips and Martin Keatman, in their 1992 book *King Arthur: The True Story*, build a systematic case for him being Enniaun Girt, whom they identify as a king of Gwynedd, in northwestern Wales. Enniaun ruled the Votadini, a people who came to the west coast of Britain from the northeast, probably an area near present-day Edinburgh, Scotland. They came to help the Britons fight off Irish invaders and stayed to establish their own kingdoms in northern Wales and Shropshire. Other investigators give the king's name, drawn from old genealogies recorded by monks, as Enniaun Yrth, with the "Yrth" corresponding to Yther or Uther. According to Phillips and Keatman, the Uther part of the name meant "terrible" or "fearsome" and Pendragon meant "head dragon," a title carried by overlords in the Votadini royal family.

The authors bestow the title of Arthur upon Pendragon's son, Owain Ddantgwyn (or Owain White-Teeth, a name that in itself suggests what might have been a legend-inspiring charisma). They cite Gildas, who in his sermon *De Excidio Britanniae* refers to Cuneglasus, Owain's son, as occupying the bear's stronghold. In the Brythonic language of the time, *arth* meant "bear." It still means "bear" in modern Welsh. Phillips and Keatman take Gildas's reference to mean that Cuneglasus inherited Arthur's stronghold, which in turn means that Arthur was Owain, Cuneglasus's father. Warriors of the time commonly adopted animal war names. The authors suggest that that Owain may have appended the Latin *ursus* to the Brythonic *arth* to form his war title—Arthursus, the bear-bear.

It should be noted that Phillips and Keatman have a fondness for attention-getting theories. Among their coauthored books is one that claims the playwright William Shakespeare led a double life as an undercover agent for Queen Elizabeth I (see chapter 9). Phillips, especially, has shown an affinity for provocative conspiracy theories in his more recent books, written without Keatman. Yet it would be unfair to throw out their case for Owain as Arthur, laid out as it is with meticulous, point-by-point reasoning. Their argument does depend on a construct of educated guesses, but so do all theories about the real Arthur. Because of the lack of information from the time, Arthurian historians are rather like those daring paleontologists who determine what a dinosaur must have looked like based on a bit of fossilized jaw, three teeth, and a thighbone.

Speaking of buried physical evidence, each theory about who Arthur really was—and there are several more besides the ones summarized in this chapter—points to archaeological finds that seem to link this personality or that with the Arthurian legend. Phillips and Keatman, for example, see the Roman city of Virconium—near present-day Wroxeter, in Shropshire—as Arthur-Owain's capital. Based on stone ruins, archaeologists once thought that the city had declined precipitously after the Romans withdrew around 400. More recent digs, however, reveal that it was rebuilt as a British stronghold later in the fifth century. Evidence of postholes shows scientists where great wooden halls stood, buildings fit for a Celtic king. In fact, the partners argue, this may have become the capital of Britain for a time, the seat of a leader powerful enough to unite other kings into an alliance.

Critics point out that Owain is generally thought to have ruled the small kingdom of Rhôs, in Northern Wales, not the separate, nearby kingdom of Powys, centered at Virconium. Yet some kings of Rhôs apparently also ruled the much larger and also adjacent kingdom of Gwynedd, and since the boundaries of these ancient kingdoms were somewhat fluid, based on shifts in power between rival kings, between fathers and sons, and between cousins and nephews, it is conceivable that Owain had a power center at Virconium.

If Owain did rule from Virconium, the authors may also be correct that an ancient fortified hill outside of Baschurch, a village in Shropshire, is the burial place of Owain. In the stories, a mortally wounded Arthur commands his marshal, Sir Bedivere, to cast Excalibur, the magical sword, into a lake. When the knight does so, a hand, that of the Lady of the Lake, reaches up from the water and catches the weapon, then draws it down into the depths. Phillips and Keatman see in that episode an echo of a pre-Christian Celtic funerary ritual, perhaps still practiced in Owain's time. It required that the deceased's belongings be cast away into water—perhaps as a sacrifice to water spirits. The authors speculate that somewhere in the mud at the bottom of Berth Pool, near the Baschurch hill, lies a sixth-century sword, waiting to be rediscovered.

Other sites associated with Arthur include a rocky outcropping called Tintagel on the north coast of Cornwall, Caerleon-on-Usk in Wales, and Cadbury Castle, the Iron Age hill fort in Somerset. Geoffrey of Monmouth mentioned Tintagel Castle as Arthur's birthplace, a claim often dismissed by twentieth-century scholars because the castle was built far too late to have welcomed a fifth- or sixth-century hero into the world. Then archaeologists found evidence of a much earlier monastery on the site, a monastery that also served as a trade center dealing in sixth-century goods from as far away as the eastern Mediterranean. Shards of imported pottery suggest that it was, if not a royal residence, at least a place associated with wealth. A piece of slate bearing the name Artognou (probably prounounced Arthnou) has also been uncovered at Tintagel.

Caerlon, the site of an ancient Roman fort, also owes its claim to Geoffrey, who lived nearby. He wrote that it was the place where Arthur held court. Caerlon, a seat of Welsh princes until the Norman Invasion, in 1066, may well have been Camelot, but there's no hard evidence.

Many locals around Cadbury believe that the ancient fortified hill belonged to Arthur, and they have held that view for many centuries—as noted by John Leyland, Henry VIII's librarian and historian, more than four hundred years ago. If the legends of a heroic Arthur actually go back to the Iron Age— perhaps as far back as 1000 BCE, as yet another school of thought has suggested—then Cadbury would be a logical place to locate Camelot. The names of two nearby towns, Queen Camel and West Camel, seem to echo an association. And although the hill's original fortifications date from the Iron Age, there is some archaeological evidence that the site was reused much later, in the sixth century CE.

Other places with "camel" in their names have also been suggested, but there's no need, really, to link the historical Arthur's city to the storied Camelot. That's because Camelot entered the Arthur stories only in the late twelfth-century poem *Lancelot, the Knight of the Cart* by the French romanticist Chrétien de Troyes. The Arthur legend, whatever its possible basis in fact, was jumbled up with fantastic Welsh folktales and ancient Celtic myths from early on. In his 1998 book *The Search for King Arthur*, poet and scholar David Day retells more than two dozen Arthurian legends—all drenched in magical elements— and traces the links between them. Arthur stories as a whole are so fantastic that one modern school of thought argues that his legend is rooted entirely in myths and fairy stories, with hardly a trace of history.

The legend gained even more layers of fantasy in the later Middle Ages and into the Renaissance as writers such as Chrétien adopted and adapted them. They blended in later Christian-inspired ideas, such as the quest for the Holy Grail. They set the tales against an anachronistic backdrop of chivalry (a concept at its height in the twelfth century) and medieval heraldry. No real Arthur or Sir Lancelot (a character invented by Chrétien) could have worn shining plate armor. Plate armor wasn't developed until centuries after Arthur's time.

The Camelot legend gained strength during eras when other ancient European folk stories fell into obscurity. This was at least in part because English monarchs adopted and promoted Arthur as a symbol of national strength and unity—ironic, since the Britons of Arthur's time were fighting Saxons and Angles, the founders of Angle-land, or England.

Kingship often required that a ruler assert his legitimacy as the chosen, the anointed one. Somewhat lacking in a direct hereditary claim to the throne, the Norman and Angevin kings of England (1066–1216) could take comfort in the partially Breton heritage of their forefather William the Conqueror. Through William's French-Breton forebears, there was perceived a connection to the Bretons' cousins, the Britons who fought under Arthur. Thus William's descendants claimed (rather presumptuously) an Arthurian right to rule the island of Britain.

In the cathedral city of Winchester, in south-central England, there is a massive round table, long purported to be Arthur's. Experts date it, however, not to the fifth or sixth century but to the reign of either King Stephen (1135–1154) or his successor Henry II (until 1189). Henry, a strong and unifying ruler, founded England's Angevin Dynasty, again a line of Norman French (and partly Breton French) kings. That probably explains why he supported the legend and approved the claim that Winchester, an important trade center during his reign, had been Arthur's Camelot. Henry may even have ordered the table built.

The medieval chronicler Gerald of Wales reported that around 1190 he witnessed the exhumation of Arthur's body from a grave at Glastonbury Abbey, in Somerset. He described a lead cross with the inscription "Here lies buried the famous King Arthur with Guinevere ... in the island of Avalon." Many modern scholars assume that the cross, its whereabouts today unknown, was a fake (although what a find it would be if it were real). Yet even if Gerald was duped, even if he fibbed, his report suggests a remarkable level of interest seven hundred years after Arthur supposedly lived.

Then much later, in 1585, Henry Tudor (Henry VII), another English king with a dubious hereditary claim, looked to his Welsh heritage for a link to Arthur and ancient legitimacy. Even Britain's modern royals wave the Athurian flag, as evidenced by the birth names of Prince Charles—Charles Philip *Arthur* George—and his son and heir, Prince William—William *Arthur* Philip Louis.

None of this establishes that Arthur was an invention, conveniently kept alive to bolster the authority of real kings. It only says that commoners and royals alike have found inspiration in King Arthur for something like fifteen hundred years. The historical records are so sketchy, however, and the dates for Arthur's battles so inconsistent, that many historians argue that he never was—that he is merely an expression of ancient British solidarity, a myth of defiance. The stories come from a period when the post-Roman Britons—Christians who viewed themselves as the legitimate heirs of a great civilization—were gradually losing their native island to encroaching Saxons, pagans whom they saw as barbarians. Their stories drafted ancient folk heroes into action as defenders of Britain.

So where does that leave the real Arthur, if he was real? It leaves him in limbo. He can't be proved. He can't be disproved. Terry Jones (the only native Welshman in the Monty Python troupe) observes in his introduction to Day's book, "For a historical figure, King Arthur seems remarkably fictional; yet for a fictional character he has had an extraordinary impact on the history of Britain."

Still, there is that archaeological evidence cited by authors Phillips and Keatman, among others—signs of a post-Roman building boom, of lucrative foreign trade. The evidence consists largely of postholes and pottery shards, yet it speaks of what might have been a "brief shining moment" in the history of late Celtic Britain.

If indeed such a "moment" (meaning a few to several decades) occurred sometime around the year 500, it could only have been the product of unity. Only united British forces could have stood fast against the Saxons. Only a unified army could have achieved a victory so decisive that it kept the enemy at bay for decades. Such unity requires a unifier. Only a strong and persuasive leader can forge a strong alliance. Whoever cobbled together the kingdoms of post-Roman Britain, joining them into so strong a confederation that the Saxons feared, at least temporarily, to attack, must have been a leader worthy of a legend. It seems only fair to call that leader, whoever he was, Arthur.

To investigate further:

Alcock, Leslie. *Arthur's Britain. History and Archaeology: A.D. 367–634.* New York: Penguin, 2002. A broad examination of research into evidence of a historical Arthur.

Ashe, Geoffrey. *The Discovery of King Arthur.* New York: Anchor Press, 1985. The author builds a case for the fifth-century leader Riothamus as the historical Arthur.

———. *The Quest for Arthur's Britain.* Chicago: Academy Chicago Publishers, 1994. An overview of the Arthur legend, as supported by archaeological evidence.

Ashley, Mike, ed. *The Mammoth Book of King Arthur: Reality and Legend, the Beginning and the End—the Most Complete Arthurian Sourcebook Ever.* New York: Carroll & Graf, 2005. The subtitle's description, "most complete sourcebook," is accurate.

Chrétien de Troyes. *Arthurian Romances*. London and New York: Dent-Dutton, 1975. A romantic, twelfth-century reimagining of Arthur stories that introduced the king's legendary capital, Camelot.

Day, David. *The Search for King Arthur*. New York: Facts on File, 1998. A beautifully illustrated examination of the legend and the possible facts behind it, with a fun introduction by Terry Jones of the Monty Python troupe.

Jenkins, Elizabeth. *The Mystery of King Arthur*. New York: Coward, McCann & Geoghegan, 1975. A thoroughly researched book, illustrated with historic artworks.

4

Did Richard III Murder the Princes in the Tower?

lthough ten of William Shakespeare's plays chronicled the history of England, Shakespeare was no historian. Sadly—at least for the reputation of King Richard III—no historian has ever been a Shakespeare, either. Published in 1597 and most likely first performed several years earlier, the play that bears the name of England's most controversial king paints an indelible portrait of evil. It's a portrait that probably bears only a passing resemblance to the real Richard III. Many writers since have tried to point this out, but Shakespeare was too good. People remember his Richard.

According to the playwright, Richard, Duke of Gloucester, was a monster, physically and morally deformed. Before he became king in 1483, this scheming hunchback supposedly killed his wife's first husband and her father, deceitfully got her to marry him, and arranged the murder of his own brother, George, Duke of Clarence. These are only a small fraction of the misdeeds attributed to him. To steal the throne for himself, Richard is supposed to have arranged for the children of his other brother, King Edward IV, to be branded as bastards (an actual legal term at the time) so that they would be barred from the line of succession. Then, after he became king, Richard is believed to have committed his most monstrous sin by ordering the murders of two of those children, his defenseless preteen nephews.

Historians have argued that the real Richard probably stood up straight and walked without a limp and may have committed none of the offenses charged to him—at least, not in the despicable context presented in the play. But the legend is too vivid; it won't fade. Besides, other historians—perhaps a majority of them over the centuries—have cared little about Richard's name being smeared. They say that Shakespeare's version, while rather loose with the physical and chronological details, may not be that far from the truth.

The playwright couldn't have made his play completely factual even if he had wanted to. He wrote during the rule of Elizabeth I. If he had crossed her, the queen would have shut down Shakespeare's theater in a heartbeat. Wisely, the poet stuck to the politically correct version of Richard III's life and reign as approved by the queen's royal line, the Tudor dynasty.

It was important for the Tudors, a foundation of their legitimacy as rulers, that Richard be forever condemned as usurper, villain, criminal—anything but a rightful king. This was because Elizabeth's grandfather, Henry Tudor, had possessed a rather shaky claim to the crown when he defeated Richard in battle and founded the dynasty. (A word of warning: This chapter contains three King Henry's—VI, VII, and VIII—and four King Edwards—III, IV, V, and VI. So watch your I's and V's.) Henry Tudor made himself King Henry VII in 1485 at the Battle of Bosworth, where Richard III was slain. (In the play, it's the scene containing the famous line "My kingdom for a horse.") The victor carried royal blood in his veins, but it had flowed through some rather remote genealogical backwaters.

In the fifteenth century's Wars of the Roses, various descendents of Edward III, who had ruled from 1327 to 1377, fought over the English crown. Henry Tudor and Richard of Gloucester were both among those descendents, an extended clan divided into dynastic factions called the Houses of Lancaster (symbolized by a red rose) and York (a white rose). Henry was a Lancastrian by way of his mother, Margaret Beaufort. She was Edward III's great-great-granddaughter, through the king's third son, John of Gaunt (whose title had been Duke of Lancaster) and his mistress, Katherine Swynford. (Gaunt later married Katherine and legitimized their children.) Richard, on the other hand, was the younger brother of the late Edward IV. Their father had been the Duke of York, descended from the daughter of Edward III's second son, Lionel, Duke of Clarence.

Henry's coronation ended the Wars of the Roses, and none too soon. Most English were happy to see the decades of bloody rivalry come to an end. The exceptions were hard-core Yorkists, who kept whipping up ineffectual rebellions that Henry had to quell. Given his vulnerabilities, Hank took care that questions about his right to rule never came up. So did his heirs—his son Henry VIII and his grandchildren Edward VI, Mary, and Elizabeth I.

Free speech and freedom of the press did not exist in Tudor England. Even more than a century after the Battle of Bosworth, Shakespeare knew it wasn't safe to write anything good about Richard III. Besides, even if Shakespeare had been interested in setting the record straight, he probably couldn't have unearthed the truth. He was working from Tudor historical sources. A history of Richard's rise and fall, authored by Sir Thomas More, was considered the most authoritative account, and it told of a hunchbacked, murderous usurper. This version was—and, in many quarters, still is—respected as honest and accurate because More is one of history's towering men of principle, a truth-teller whose soul, Erasmus said, "was more pure than any snow." More is remembered as the English chancellor who refused to acknowledge Henry VIII as self-appointed head of the English Church. In return, the king executed More for treason in 1535. Four hundred years later, Pope Pius XI canonized him as Saint Thomas More.

More's account of Richard's murderous rise to power and malevolent reign, written in Latin and English, probably served as a source for Raphael Holinshed's *Chronicle*, published in 1577 as the official history of England. The *Chronicle* was one of Shakespeare's favorite sources. Yet More, the supposed authority, had no firsthand knowledge of Richard III. He was a little boy when Richard died at Bosworth and Henry VII took the throne. In addition, More never finished his historiography of Richard and never tried to publish it. It was published after he died.

Modern historian Bertram Fields is among many today who think that More, like Shakespeare, didn't really know what he was writing about. Fields points out that More grew up in the household of John Morton, the archbishop of Canterbury. Morton had been one of Richard III's bitterest enemies and helped to plan an unsuccessful uprising against him. Once Richard was out of the way, Morton thrived under Henry VII. Fields suggests that the young and impressionable More was simply writing down what Morton had told him about the hated Richard. More may even have been copying out an earlier history that Morton had written. Fields thinks it likely that More abandoned the project because he looked more thoroughly into his subject matter and realized that Morton had lied.

Fields's theory is speculation, but so is much of what's thought about the real Richard. Writers going back at least as far as Horace Walpole in the eighteenth century have tried to paint a clearer picture of the man, working from thin evidence. Most agree that no reliable account from Richard's lifetime describes a hump on his back or his other supposed deformity, a withered arm. One portrait, reputedly painted from life, shows one shoulder higher than the other, but a twentieth-century X-ray revealed that the original painting depicted the shoulders as level and normal. A later touchup added the asymmetry.

Contemporary accounts do mention Richard's skill as a warrior and that he was remarkably strong for his size. They also name his favored weapon. It's hard to imagine a small man (probably about five foot, six inches) with a bent spine and a withered arm wielding a heavy battle-ax while keeping his horse under control amid bloody chaos.

As for Richard's crimes, the evidence is largely hearsay. He probably did some of the nasty things attributed to him, but even in those cases, the surrounding circumstances may have been changed by Tudor-era writers to make him sound worse than he was.

Richard's wife, Anne, was the daughter of the Earl of Warwick, who died in a 1471 battle against the forces of Edward IV, Richard's big brother. Her first husband was the Prince of Wales and an heir apparent to the crown (as the son of Henry VI, Edward's predecessor). The prince also died in battle against Edward, so perhaps Anne would have resented Richard, who had fought on Edward's side (but had not, as far as history records, delivered the fatal blows to either the Earl of Warwick or the Prince of Wales).

Maybe Richard had to trick Anne or force her to marry him, but not necessarily. Anne and Richard had been friends from childhood, when he had lived in her father's household. Alliances shifted quickly and radically among these noble families. The Earl of Warwick was called "Kingmaker" because he had successfully fought to oust the pious but feeble-minded Henry VI and put Edward IV on the throne in 1461. The Earl of

Warwick later turned against Edward and drove him into exile in 1470, reinstalling Henry VI, who was by then insane (and thus not likely to get in the Earl of Warwick's way). When Anne's father and husband died in battle, they were fighting to keep Edward from regaining the throne, an effort in which they failed.

It's not unlikely, then, that just as her father had switched alliances, Anne decided she was better off hitching her fortunes to those of her old friend Richard, one of England's most powerful nobles again, now that his brother was back on the throne.

Edward and Richard had another brother, George, the Duke of Clarence, who, like the Earl of Warwick, was fickle in his loyalties and a rebel. Shakespeare depicts Richard convincing Edward to charge brother George with treason. Then the playwright shows George murdered (drowned in a vat of wine) by Richard's paid henchmen. But it was almost certainly Edward who ordered the disloyal and unpredictable George to be executed. Richard's role in the matter is unclear. The same goes for the killing of Henry VI, another dastardly deed often pinned on Richard alone. Edward had been knocked off his throne in 1470 by Warwick and Lancastrian partisans who were eager to prop up the crazy old king and use him as a figurehead. Edward decided that Henry VI—although only a harmless lunatic—had to die so that it couldn't happen again. Did Edward personally kill him? Did loyal brother Richard do the dirty work or order it done? It's hard to say. Both of the brothers probably saw the ousted king's death as a matter of national necessity—a regrettably bloody way to settle unrest and avoid future uprisings.

Edward IV ruled for another decade and then died unexpectedly of an illness in 1483, just short of his forty-first birthday. (No one has suggested that Richard had anything to do with *that* death.) King Edward, in his will, specified that if he were to die while his heir, a son who was also named Edward, was still too young to rule, Richard would act as protector—the de facto ruler of England and guardian of Edward V—until such time as the young king was ready to wield power on his own. When his father died, Edward V was only twelve, which meant that Richard—at least temporarily—was in charge.

It seemed a good plan, but conflict immediately arose. The prince had been growing up under the care of his mother's family, the Woodvilles. They had been a clan of low rank and little wealth until Elizabeth Woodville, a beautiful, flaxen-haired widow, married the king (known for his amorous appetites) in 1464. The marriage enraged Warwick, who had been trying to arrange a match between Edward and a French princess. Other nobles disliked the marriage because they hated seeing the no-account Woodville (also spelled Wydville) bunch cozy up to such power and wealth.

As queen consort, Elizabeth had ambitiously secured high offices and titles for many of her avaricious relatives, earning the family, and Edward, a great deal of resentment. It led to Warwick's rebellion and resulted in Edward's 1470–1471 exile.

Once Edward had regained power, he continued to let his upstart in-laws improve their fortunes, often at the expense of other, higher-born nobles. When Edward suddenly died, the Woodvilles saw a further opportunity to amass power, by controlling the new king.

Richard prevented this. He intercepted the Woodville contingent as they escorted young Edward V to London for coronation. Richard arrested Earl Rivers (the queen's brother), and Richard Grey (her grown son by her first marriage) and took nephew Eddie into protective custody. He housed the boy in the Tower of London, which at the time was still a royal residence and not just a prison. The protector vowed his loyalty to the new king and directed preparations for Edward V's coronation.

Before the big day, something changed. Exercising his authority as Lord Protector, Richard ordered the arrest of Lord Hastings, his brother's trusted, longtime chancellor and a frequent visitor to the new King Edward in the tower. The official story is that Richard ordered Hastings seized and taken immediately to the Tower green, where he was beheaded. Another version says that Hastings was duly tried and convicted of treason before the execution.

Richard accused Hastings of plotting with Edward IV's widow, Elizabeth, and her Woodville relatives to wrest away control of the new king and the country. Richard ordered more beheadings, including those of Rivers and Grey—the uncle and the half-brother, respectively, of the young king Edward V. Inexplicably, Elizabeth allowed her other young son, a nine-year-old also named Richard, to stay with his brother at the Tower, under their uncle's care. Was she coerced, or did she know something about her former brother-in-law's character that caused her to assume the boys would be safe? What happened to little Eddie and Richie from then on is unknown—except that Edward V never had his coronation.

Instead, Richard of Gloucester was crowned King Richard III of England. The switcheroo was helped along by a statute of Parliament called the Titulus Regius. Under Titulus Regius, the members ruled that the 1464 marriage of Edward IV to Elizabeth Woodville had been illegal, and that the couple's children together—including young Edward and Richard—were illegitimate. Thus their uncle, Richard of Gloucester, was the next legitimate successor.

How did Parliament reach such a conclusion? Robert Stillington, a churchman who was bishop of Bath and Wells, had come forward to say that in 1461, Edward IV had agreed to marry another woman, one Eleanor Butler. Such an agreement, called a "precontract," was like a betrothal, and it had all the legal standing of a marriage. Thus, Edward had not been free to marry Elizabeth three years later.

Was Stillington's story true? Had Richard or one of his allies put the bishop up to it? Was this a trumped-up way for Richard to seize power? The bishop supposedly showed evidence of the precontract to Richard, the royal council, and Parliament.

Lady Eleanor had died in 1468, so no one could check the facts with her. Edward IV had always displayed a weakness for pretty women, and it would have been just like him to promise a woman anything, even marriage, so he could get what he wanted from her. But just because it sounds likely doesn't make it the truth.

It is also entirely possible that Parliament was looking for any excuse not to crown a twelve-year-old as king, and that Stillington conveniently provided such an excuse. A minor on the throne tended to be trouble. Foreign powers often judged a country ruled by a child to be weak, a good target for invasion. Besides that, there were plenty of nobles appalled at the prospect of young Edward V, once he reached majority, doing the bidding of his Woodville cousins.

Once Richard had the crown for himself, it might have made sense for him to eliminate his nephews. Just as Parliament had declared them bastards, it could later have reversed itself and declared them legitimate heirs to the crown. (In fact, it later did just that.) For Richard, it would have been safer to have them out of the way. Among these warring noble families, killing a potential rival for the crown was not terribly unusual. Case in point: old Henry VI.

Richard's latter-day defenders point out, however, that there is no firm proof that anyone killed the boys. It's just that they were never heard from again. Did they go into hiding? Some theorists believe that they were spirited away for their own safety, and they grew up under assumed identities. (For more about that, see the next chapter.) Even if they were murdered, there are suspects other than Richard. They include his ally the Duke of Buckingham, who might have urged, ordered, or even committed the murders out of overzealousness. Buckingham, who also had a hereditary claim to the crown, could even have been clearing the way for a takeover of his own.

Just as the best portrait of an evil Richard is contained in a work of literature—that is, Shakespeare's play—the best, or at least the most entertaining, counterargument takes the form of a 1951 novella by Josephine Tey. In *Daughter of Time*, a bedridden police detective overcomes boredom by tackling the mystery of the little princes. He concludes that Richard didn't do it. The policeman's suspect of choice: Henry VII. Inspector Grant of Scotland Yard pounces on the absence of any official mention that the boys had gone missing—especially after Henry took possession of the Tower in 1485. Wouldn't foes of the late King Richard have been shocked and horrified not to find the boys? Wouldn't the new King Henry raise a ruckus and launch an investigation?

Not necessarily, Grant decides. Consider that the boys were even more dangerous rivals to Henry VII than they had been to their uncle. To shore up his tenuous claim to kingship, Henry arranged to marry Elizabeth of York, the daughter of the late Edward IV and Elizabeth Woodville. Young Liz was also a sister of the presumably missing Edward V. The political advantage of Henry's marriage would be null, however, if Elizabeth continued to be considered illegitimate. So, Henry had the Titulus Regius repealed and ordered the original document and any copies to be destroyed.

Author Tey's fictional inspector sees the murder of the boys as hinging on that reversal. With the Titulus Regius lifted, Edward V would again have been the rightful king. It would have been Henry, then, who needed the boy and his brother, second in the line of succession, to disappear. Under this scenario, there would have been witnesses—servants, at the least—who would have known that the boys had been alive and well when Richard last rode away to do battle. It would not have been in Henry VII's interest to call attention to their subsequent absence. Thus, no alarm was raised.

Does that theory clear Richard III of the murders? No. It has a major flaw, in that tradition says the boys disappeared in 1483 and that their deaths were rumored late that year, well before Henry took over in 1485. In fact, the charge that Richard murdered "babies" helped his opponents to foment rebellion against him.

In 1502, Henry VII ordered the execution of Sir James Tyrrell, the governor of Guisnes Castle, the fortress that guarded the English-held port of Calais, France. The crime: harboring a traitor. According to More, Tyrrell confessed before his execution that he had killed the boys almost two decades earlier—at the behest of his then master, Richard III. There are problems with this reported "confession," however. For one thing, it is mentioned in no other source. More also wrote that King Richard had not known Tyrrell before ordering him to kill the boys and that Richard granted a knighthood to Tyrrell for his loyal commission of the double murder. Neither claim can be true. The princes were last reported alive in 1483, whereas Tyrrell became a knight the previous year, a reward for his service fighting under Richard's command in England's wars against Scotland.

Finally, any confession from Tyrrell came under torture. Some supposed military intelligence authorities, even as late as the early twenty-first century, have argued that valuable truths can be discovered through torture—that pain elicits cooperation. Other experts argue that any information obtained under duress must necessarily be considered suspect—that a torture victim will say whatever his tormentors want him to say in order to stop the pain.

According to historian Fields, any modern court of law would find insufficient evidence to judge Richard guilty. Modern mock trials, hosted by the Richard III Society (an organization of history buffs who advocate for rehabilitation of the monarch's reputation), have repeatedly failed to convict.

Many historians, among them the popular writer Alison Weir, firmly believe that the circumstances surrounding Richard's accession to the throne are damning enough—maybe not for a court of law, but for the court of history. The Regius Titulus was a bald-faced contrivance, they say, and it left too many English subjects unconvinced. That was why Richard had to kill the boys. If this is true, the murders only forestalled the usurper king's inevitable fall at Bosworth Field—and not by very long, either. He reigned only a little more than two years.

In 1674, workers repairing a stairwell of the Garden Tower, part of the Tower of London complex, dug up a wooden box containing two smallish skeletons that appeared to be those of boys. On the chance that these were the remains of Edward V and his brother Richard, King Charles II ordered them put in an urn and interred in Westminster Abbey. In 1933, the bones were taken out so that a group of physicians and dentists could examine them. The skeletons were incomplete, but they did appear to be from children about the same ages that the boys were when they disappeared. Beyond that, the examiners drew few conclusions, not even identifying either skeleton's gender before the bones were returned to the tomb.

It is almost certain that modern scientists armed with twenty-first-century technology could learn much more, if Buckingham Palace ever granted permission for the remains again to be disturbed. DNA testing conceivably could confirm that the deceased were royals. Testing for the identity of the remains might also require that the remains of Edward IV, the father of the princes, or Elizabeth Woodville, their mother, be disinterred for genetic comparison. (Both lie in the chapel of Windsor Castle.) Criminal forensic techniques might even reveal what caused the boys' deaths, although that may be too much to ask. Legend says the boys were smothered in their beds.

Queen Elizabeth II steadfastly has denied permission for more testing, preferring to let the remains rest in peace. Perhaps one of her successors will judge it more important to learn the truth. Yet there is only so much truth that the bones can tell.

Even if they could be proved, definitively, to belong to young Edward and young Richard, and even if they could somehow show that the boys had died of foul play (a long shot), it is almost certain that they could not point a fleshless distal phalanx (that is, a finger bone) at the guilty party.

So what are we to think of poor Richard III, all these centuries later? During his short reign, he was a reformer and a competent administrator. Unlike his libertine brother, Edward IV, he appears to have been pious and perhaps a bit prudish, yet historians such as Fields find, in examining his writings, a wry sense of humor and a forgiving nature. Would such qualities go hand in hand with cold-blooded murder?

The answer is no, although the definition of murder may have been mitigated by what a king saw as the need to achieve order and eliminate challenges to his authority. The majority of modern historians believe that Richard murdered his nephews, if only because they disappeared while in his custody and he seemed to have the most to gain from their deaths. Yet the Tudor monarchs and their friends went to such lengths in painting Richard as a monstrous villain that, to paraphrase a line from another Shakespeare play, methinks they do protest too much. If the existence of a hump on Richard's back was fabricated, maybe the murders were, too. Although this mystery may never be solved, it seems only fair to give Richard III a wary benefit of the doubt.

To investigate further:

Chrimes, S. B. *Henry VII*. Berkeley: University of California Press, 1971. An in-depth, scholarly biography of Richard III's enemy and successor.

Cunningham, Sean. *Richard III: A Royal Enigma*. London: National Archives, 2004. Reproductions of original documents from Richard's rule, put in context by the author's narrative.

Fields, Bertram. *Royal Blood: Richard III and the Mystery of the Princes*. New York: ReaganBooks, 1998. The author, a lawyer, cross-examines history to contradict traditional tellings of the Richard story.

Harvey, Nancy Lenz. *Elizabeth of York: The Mother of Henry VIII*. New York: Macmillan, 1973. A biography of Richard III's niece, who married his enemy and successor.

Hicks, Michael. *Richard III*. Stroud, Gloustershire, UK: Tempus Publishing, 2004. The author examines the king as a politician in a time of lies and counter-lies.

Jenkins, Elizabeth. *The Princes in the Tower*. New York: Coward, McCann & Geoghegan, 1978. The author presents history with a literary flair. Highly readable.

Kendall, Paul Murray. *Richard the Third*. New York: W. W. Norton, 1975. An entertaining and accessible introduction to the man and the controversies surrounding him.

Seward, Desmond. *Richard III: England's Black Legend*. New York: Franklin Watts, 1984. The biographer makes a case against the king, countering attempts to rehabilitate his reputation.

St. Aubyn, Giles. *The Year of Three Kings: 1483*. New York: Atheneum, 1983. The author interweaves disparate events in a momentous year.

Tey, Josephine. *Four, Five, and Six by Tey (The Singing Sands, A Shilling for Candles, The Daughter of Time)*. New York: Macmillan, 1952. The novelist sets a fictional detective to work on a real historical case.

Weir, Alison. *The Princes in the Tower*. New York: Ballantine, 1992. A leading popular historian makes a compelling case for Richard's guilt in the murders of his nephews.

5

Perkin Warbeck: Pretend Pretender or Real Royal?

I n the 1993 movie *Dave*, a regular guy masquerades so successfully as the president of the United States that he's able to take over the government. Of course, this could never happen in real life, but in the 1490s a case of assumed identity almost as preposterous really did take place in Europe. A young man who looked uncannily like the late king Edward IV of England successfully passed himself off as a prince, apparently fooling the rulers of France, Scotland, and the Holy Roman Empire, among others. Royals welcomed him as a kinsman, entertained him in their courts, and supported his military expeditions. Scotland's James IV even arranged a marriage for him. The bride was the king's cousin.

Dave's title character, played by Kevin Kline, is a kindly employment agent who bears a physical resemblance to President Bill Mitchell. Taking advantage of the likeness, he makes appearances at grand openings and such, as a small-time impersonator.

This side job attracts the attention of White House staff. They enlist Dave as a presidential double and use him to mask the real president's comings and goings. After Mitchell suffers a stroke and falls into a coma, the scheming White House chief of staff (Frank Langella) installs Dave as a puppet stand-in president, intending to take all the power into his own evil hands. The movie is a comedy so, of course, nice-guy Dave turns the tables on the corrupt chief of staff and saves America. He even ends up with first lady Sigourney Weaver.

By contrast, the career of royal impersonator Perkin Warbeck—if that was his name—was a tragic farce. It ended with Perkin at the end of a rope.

Perkin the pretender enters historical accounts in 1491, about six years into the reign of England's Henry VII (introduced in the previous chapter). The word *pretender* in this context doesn't mean someone playing make-believe. It applies to a person who claims a legitimate right to a throne.

England's Wars of the Roses—a decades-long power struggle between the royal houses of Lancaster and York—ended when Richard III died fighting Henry Tudor's army in 1485. Henry, of the Lancasters (peripherally, on his mother's side), seized the crown. To hedge his bet, he married a House of York princess, the daughter of the late Edward IV. Their children, at least, would be descendants of both houses.

Family feuds die hard. Staunch Yorkists seethed with resentment toward Henry. Some of them hatched plots to unseat him. Perkin Warbeck's claim to be a long-lost son of the House of York is thought to have been just such a plot, and not the first.

Early in Henry's reign, an Oxford priest named Richard Symonds (or perhaps Roger Simon) noticed that a local boy, Lambert Simnel, looked a bit like Edward IV. There was nothing royal about ten-year-old Lambert, the son of a tradesman, but Symonds, a Yorkist sympathizer, schooled the child in speech and manners and began to introduce him around as Richard of Shrewsbury, the younger son of the late king. The real Richard of Shrewsbury, also called the Duke of York, and his older brother (who had briefly been Edward V) disappeared mysteriously when they were ten and twelve years old, respectively. They were presumed dead (the topic of the previous chapter). Perhaps Symonds thought that young Prince Richard had been too well-known, because he soon altered his scheme. The priest decided instead to pass off Simnel as twelve-year-old Edward Plantagenet, the Earl of Warwick. Young Edward's late father, George, the Duke of Clarence, was brother to both Richard III and Edward IV. Next to the princes in the Tower, the Earl of Warwick had the strongest of Yorkist claims to the crown.

Symonds took Lambert across the Irish Sea in 1487 to meet with other supporters of the House of York. In Dublin Cathedral, the partisans held a coronation, crowning the boy Edward VI. King Henry possessed an excellent counterargument in the person of the genuine article—Edward, Earl of Warwick. The king, acutely aware of young Edward's claim to the throne, had been keeping that boy, his wife's cousin, locked up in the Tower of London. It was easy enough to parade the real Earl of Warwick through the city streets, a living demonstration that Lambert Simnel was a fake.

Lambert's supporters pushed on anyway, landing an invasion force composed mainly of German mercenaries (paid for by the Duchess of Burgundy, another member of the York clan) in June. The king's army prevailed decisively at the Battle of Stoke, taking the pretender prisoner. Rather than beheading the boy for treason or jailing him, Henry took pity on Lambert and let him have a job as a servant in the palace kitchen.

The story of Perkin Warbeck is nowhere near as neat as that of Lambert Simnel. Mainstream history insists that Perkin was also an imposter—the son of a Flemish boatman or, in slightly different accounts, the son of a customs taker or a gatekeeper.

The young man himself signed a confession, just before Henry hanged him, admitting that he was an uneducated wanderer from Flanders who had been pressed into the role of royal pretender by a group of people on a dockside in Cork, Ireland. Apparently, he had begun life as one Piers Osbeck or Pierquin Wesbecque (or some other variation on the name), the son of Jehan Wesbecque in the port city of Tournai (now in Belgium).

Piers or Pierquin or Perkin supposedly spent his rootless youth among relatives in Flanders. After a brief, aborted stint as an apprentice to a cloth merchant, he ran away and attached himself to an English family, becoming their servant and traveling with them to Portugal. After serving for a short time as squire to a knight, he sailed from Lisbon to Ireland with his next employer, Pregent Meno, a merchant from Brittany.

The crucial part of the official story is set upon the waterfront of Cork, where Perkin, traveling with Meno, debarks from a ship dressed in fine silks. A group of locals, struck by his handsome looks and bearing, takes him for a noble and asks whether he is Edward, the Earl of Warwick (the same Edward that Lambert Simnel had pretended to be). When Perkin tells them he is not, they suggest that he is instead John of Gloucester, the bastard son of the late Richard III. After Perkin also denies that identity, they decide he must be the missing Richard, the Duke of York. Perkin again demurs, but the crowd insists until he agrees that, all right, if these kind people so desire him to be Prince Richard, then that's who he will be.

Upon this unlikely sounding episode was founded the rest of the young man's life. Urged on by complete strangers, this uneducated Fleming switched identities and transformed himself into an English prince—one who had mysteriously disappeared. And he did it so perfectly that he quickly became a credible challenger to the sitting king.

Obviously, it didn't happen that way. Variations on the story give Perkin a bit more education. For example, Sir Edward

Brampton—who knew the pretender well—wrote a version in which Perkin had trained as a musician and spent years as a squire in Portugal. Yet no conventional account exists that entirely explains how Perkin, if that is who he was, could have become as convincing a Richard as he apparently did

In 1616, Thomas Gainsford wrote *The True and Wonderful History of Perkin Warbeck*, the first of many writings over the centuries arguing that the pretender was what he claimed to be, the real Duke of York. If he was not, then his transformation seems to have been far beyond masquerade. It was an invention of self—an intriguing subject that has drawn the interest of artists as well as historians. Both seventeenth-century playwright John Ford and nineteenth-century novelist Mary Wollstonecraft Shelley wrote their own reimagined versions of his story, and both treated Perkin sympathetically.

In the twenty-first century, historian Ann Wroe argues persuasively in her book *The Perfect Prince* that the pretender's true identity and origins remain a mystery. She argues that several things about the official version of Perkins's story make no sense. Take, for example, the silks that Perkin wore on the dockside in Cork. Supposedly, they belonged to Perkin's "master," Meno. Why would a Breton merchant own this finery? In what context would he wear it? In many tellings, the silks are Meno's wares, his merchandise, and the handsome young Perkin is modeling them to drum up sales. Wroe argues that this is preposterous because there was no market for fine cloth at the Cork waterside. Her research has revealed that Meno dealt not in fine cloth but in fleeces, sheepskins.

She further notes that when Perkin showed up in Cork, there was nothing accidental or serendipitous about his appearance. John Atwater, the mayor of Cork, had been expecting the young man and was there to receive him formally as a claimant to the English crown. The earls of Desmond and Kildare, both York supporters, attended, as did one John Taylor, the commander of a small fleet of ships. Wroe reports that Taylor had brought with him a newly made suit of white armor, fit for a prince and a perfect fit for the young man from Portugal.

Prince Richard, as he was now known, told sympathetic listeners that when he was a little boy in the Tower of London, men came to kill him and his older brother, the sometime Edward V. He did not know who had sent the men. Although Edward had been murdered, the man assigned to kill Richard had found himself unable to commit such a dastardly crime. Taking pity, he had smuggled Richard away and helped him get to safety on the European continent, where the boy had grown up in hiding.

Whether the crowd believed that story or simply welcomed any rival to Henry VII, the monarchs of Europe proved receptive—many of them, anyway. Richard soon received an invitation to stay at the court of Charles V of France. There the young man received full honors due a visiting prince. He met with Maximilian I, the Grand Duke of Austria and soon to be the Holy Roman Emperor. The courts of Denmark and Sweden sent word that they supported Richard's claim to England's crown.

Richard's most fervent support came from Margaret of York, the widow of the Duke of Burgundy. The dowager duchess welcomed Richard as her nephew, the son of her late brother, Edward IV. She said that the young man's birthmarks proved his identity. She confirmed his childhood memories of English court life.

Of course, Margaret had also backed the claim of Lambert Simnel, clearly a fake and now scrubbing pots. She hated Henry and appeared ready to attack him with any old pretender who was handy. Not only had Henry stolen the throne from her other brother, Richard III, he had also failed to pay money owed by the English crown to the Duchy of Burgundy and had confiscated York family lands. Above all, Margaret hated the English king as a Lancastrian sitting on a throne that she considered rightfully to belong to the House of York.

Margaret and Maximilian supplied Richard with fourteen ships, men, weapons, and money for an invasion of England. The young prince personally took command of the fleet, landing near the port of Deal (north of Dover on England's southeast coast) in July 1495. The plan was to drum up popular support and increase the size of his force, which was made up—as had been Lambert Simnel's—of mercenaries, their loyalty far from guaranteed. When the locals saw these rough adventurers and realized there were no English nobles of any power or prestige traveling with the prince, they knew better than to turn against their powerful and vengeful king. A small advance force of Richard's men ventured ashore and died in a brutal slaughter. The prince gave up and sailed away.

Richard sought and received support and welcome from James IV of Scotland. The Scots and the English were longtime enemies, and James eagerly listened to plans for overthrowing Henry. During Richard's lengthy stay at the court in Edinburgh, James granted a generous monthly pension to his guest and also introduced Richard to Lady Katharine Gordon. She was the king's cousin and was descended from a duke, a fit wife for a prince. Richard asked for and received the king's blessing to marry Katherine.

In the early fall of 1496, Richard again mounted an invasion force. With an ill-trained army of fourteen hundred men, he crossed from Scotland into the English county of Northumberland. The incursion lasted three days, during which Richard's forces pillaged and killed locals—not a very good way to drum up support for a revolution. Without encountering English forces, they withdrew. The attack had been another pitiful failure, an embarrassment. Richard had worn out his welcome.

Richard and Katherine sailed from Scotland to Cork, where he expected to find supporters again but did not. Leaving his wife in Ireland, he took two ships and a small force of men and sailed for Cornwall. Apparently having learned from experience, Richard this time appealed to the locals with promises that as king he would cut their taxes. That worked, and he gathered a force of a few thousand as he marched eastward. Near Exeter in Devon, his followers hailed him as King Richard IV.

The triumph was minor and brief. When his supporters, few of them armed with anything beyond sticks and daggers, met Henry's army, they turned and fled, as did "Richard IV." He surrendered at an abbey in Hampshire and was taken prisoner. Henry took him to London and paraded him through the streets so that the citizens could mock him.

Oddly, Henry housed his prisoner not in the Tower of London but at Westminster, where he was given the treatment usually reserved for royal guests. Instead of thanking Henry for being lenient, Richard ran away. Henry's guards caught him the same day. The king threw the pretender in the stocks, exposing him to more ridicule. Then he sent him to the Tower—the place from which, supposedly, he had escaped as a boy. The guards put him in the cell next to one where Edward Plantagenet, the Earl of Warwick, was locked up. It's not known whether the Earl of Warwick believed that the prisoner next door was his cousin, but the two young men, now both in their mid-twenties, hit it off. Together with one of the jailers—a Duke of Warwick supporter—they plotted an escape. The plan involved burning down the Tower of London and staging a coup.

Through an informer, the king found out about the plot. He charged Richard, the Earl of Warwick, the jailer, and other conspirators with treason and sentenced them to death. As historian Wroe points out, this was a curious charge when applied to Richard. The name Perkin Warbeck was what Henry called the young pretender. (It's not known whether anyone else ever called him by that name.) The king supplied the details of the confession that Richard was coerced to read aloud and sign before he died. If the prisoner was really from Flanders, as Henry insisted, then he was a subject not of the king of England but of Mary of Burgundy (Margaret's stepdaughter) and her husband, Holy Roman Emperor Maximilian I. Treason—then defined as disloyalty toward or betrayal of one's sovereign—would not apply.

It was a lot tougher back then to get off on a technicality. On November 23, 1499, Richard (or Perkin or whoever) was hanged to death on the public gallows at the nearby village of Tyburn (now part of London). About a week later, Edward was beheaded at the Tower. Henry ordered copies of the confession distributed and read publicly throughout England. He and his Tudor heirs went on to rule through the following century.

So who was the man who died under the name Perkin Warbeck? Is there any chance he was who he said he was, Richard of Shrewsbury, the Duke of York? Most historians don't think so, but there is this: if a merciful executioner had indeed taken pity on young Richard, sneaked him out of the Tower, and sent him to the continent, there would be no more likely place to stash the boy than in the Belgian court. Could those royal manners and bearing have been gained by growing up in the household of his aunt, Margaret of York? And what does it mean that Henry at first treated his prisoner as a guest? Could there be in that gesture any acknowledgment that this was, or perhaps could have been, a legitimate royal? Remember, Henry was married to Edward IV's daughter. The real Richard would have been the king's brother-in-law.

Perkin's claim rested, at least initially, on the strong resemblance he bore to the late Edward IV, the father of Richard. Edward had fathered ten children by his wife Elizabeth Woodville, but he also sired at least six illegitimate children. Given his character, there may well have been a few more. It's even conceivable (pun intended) that Lambert Simnel was one of Edward's bastards. Edward generally did right by his out-of-wedlock progeny, so he might have placed the child in a noble household to be raised. Again, the household of Edward's sister in Belgium would have been a likely place for her brother's son to grow up.

Could Perkin have been no more than Henry VII said he was—an uneducated son of an uneducated Flemish boatman? This seems the least likely possibility, although it's widely accepted as truth. Ann Wroe points out that the archives of Tournai, where official records of the time were kept, burned up during a German bomber attack in World War II, closing that avenue of inquiry.

It seems that the only way that a poor boy with no education could have moved among royals with the grace and self-assurance that this young man apparently did would be if he had been taken up and raised in a noble household. Again, the most likely of such households would be the royal court of Belgium. Margaret of York, the widow of the duke of Belgium, is known to have played a major role in the brief and tragic career of Perkin/Richard. Very likely, she played an even greater role than is known. Somehow, her protégé received extensive training, probably well before he ever appeared beside that ship in Cork.

What if Perkin/Richard had succeeded? What if he had secured the crown? Did those who supported him think he had a chance of winning? And if he had won, would they have been content to let him rule, or was there someone like Frank Langella in the movie Dave lurking about, someone who intended to wield power through the inexperienced king? Wroe suggests that the greatest evidence that the pretender was the real thing is that his backers backed him—not because they thought he was a great military leader (he apparently was not), and not because they expected to control England through him, but because they thought it was the right thing to do.

To investigate further:

Arthurson, Ian. *The Perkin Warbeck Conspiracy: 1491–1499*. Stroud, Gloucestershire, UK: Sutton Publishing, 1993. Traces how the pretender's claim changed European politics.

Bayley, John. *The History and Antiquities of the Tower of London*. London: Jennings & Chaplin, 1830. A lavishly illustrated story of the Tower's long history as a fort, a palace, and a prison.

Ford, John. *'Tis Pity She's a Whore and Other Plays: The Lover's Melancholy; The Broken Heart; 'Tis Pity She's a Whore; Perkin Warbeck*. New York: Oxford University Press, 1999. A vintage English play dramatizes the life of the pretender to the throne.

Gairdner, James. *History of the Life and Reign of Richard the Third: To Which Is Added the Story of Perkin Warbeck from Original Documents*. Boston: Adamant, 2000. The long subtitle describes this one.

Hume, Robert: *Who Was . . . Perkin Warbeck: The Boy Who Would Be King*. London: Short Books, 2005. The author takes a few liberties in writing an accessible story aimed at younger readers.

Kleyn, Diana. *Richard of England*. Bourne End, Buckinghamshire, UK: Kensal Press, 1991. The author compares what she portrays as the parallel lives of Richard of York and Perkin Warbeck. The appendix includes original documents.

Potter, Jeremy. *Pretenders to the English Crown*. Lanham, MD: Barnes & Noble Imports, 1987. The author reviews the stories of those who failed in their quests for the throne.

Shelley, Mary Wollstonecraft. *The Fortunes of Perkin Warbeck: A Romance*. Whitefish, MT: Kessinger, 2004. A fictionalized telling of the Warbeck story by an author better known for her *Frankenstein*.

Wroe, Ann. *The Perfect Prince: The Mystery of Perkin Warbeck and His Quest for the Throne of England*. New York: Random House, 2003. This overwrought but meticulous narrative makes the case that Warbeck was more than most historians believe.

6

Did Henry VIII Doom the Tudor Dynasty with Syphilis?

A wound on his leg became a festering sore that wouldn't heal. Ulcers spread over his legs and feet. Already burly, the aging English king became grossly obese and then swelled up even further with dropsy. As he did, his toes turned gangrenous. His teeth rotted, his gums bled, his breath stank. Latter-day diagnosticians have put forward many theories for what was wrong, including advanced diabetes and a severe vitamin deficiency. So what's with the widely circulated notion that Henry VIII's dramatic mental and emotional deterioration at the end of his life indicated tertiary syphilis?

The answer to that question is all tied up with "the King's great matter," as it was euphemistically termed in early 1530s England. The "matter" was Henry VIII's determination to annul his marriage of twenty-four years so that he could wed a younger, hotter, and presumably more fertile woman.

The king's great matter sounds more like a midlife crisis than statecraft to modern ears. Yet Henry was not merely horny. The king wanted a son, a male heir. More than wanted—he needed one. Henry felt it imperative that he produce a male heir if the Tudor dynasty was to survive and England to avoid another bloody civil war such as the Wars of the Roses, the dragged-out series of conflicts that his father, Henry VII, had ended when he won the Battle of Bosworth Field in 1485 and seized the crown.

Between 1509, when Henry and Catharine of Aragon married, and 1518, Catherine had been pregnant six or seven times. Only one child, Mary, had survived. There was no law in England (as there was in France) that said a female could not ascend to the throne, but neither was it considered certain that the English would fully embrace a ruling queen. And Henry knew that other European monarchs were far more likely to attempt an invasion after his death if they perceived a vulnerable leader, one with less than complete support from the English nobles. A male heir seemed an urgent national priority.

In late 1525, Catherine turned forty; Henry was only thirty-four. The likelihood that she could bear him a healthy son was dwindling. It dwindled to nothing as he spent less time with her over the late 1520s. He had noticed a fascinating young woman among Catherine's ladies-in-waiting, the dark-eyed Anne Boleyn. The royal stallion decided to try his luck with a fresh mare.

Henry had already fathered a son (Henry Fitzroy) by a mistress. He didn't need another bastard; he needed a legitimate heir. So the king took steps—extreme steps—to see that his marriage to Catherine was dissolved and his marriage to Anne ruled legal. This involved getting Parliament to declare him supreme head of the (English) church, thus bringing about the English Reformation. But that's a separate story.

As the guitar-playing philosopher John Hiatt said, "Once true love's departed, you do it over and over again." In all, there would be six wives. Two of them Henry cast off because they did not suit either his needs (the first) or his fancy (the fourth). Another two (the second and the fifth) he ordered beheaded. The third wife, the only one who gave him a surviving son (Edward VI), died of an infection contracted in childbirth. Henry's sixth wife survived him. The total output in offspring (those surviving infancy) from all these unions: three—Edward and two daughters, Mary and Elizabeth (the latter by Anne Boleyn). All of them would wear the crown—first Edward, then Mary, then Elizabeth—but none would produce a direct heir of his or her own. The Tudor dynasty would die with Elizabeth in 1603. Her cousin, Henry's great-grandnephew James VI of Scotland, would inherit the throne, becoming James I of England and bringing the House of Stuart to the southern half of the great British island.

Henry still looms so large in the popular imagination—larger, surely than any other English monarch—for the story of this matrimonial parade and how it changed England. His oversized persona also endures because he *was* so large. Tall and physically imposing even as a prince, Henry swelled to gross dimensions during the span of his reign. His waist size increased by seventeen inches in one year. Eventually, his chest measured fifty-seven inches, and three men of average size could fit inside one of his tunics.

The memorable bits add up to a simplified image of a gluttonous, lustful, willful despot. Henry, who ruled England from 1509 to 1547, was all of those things. He also was a mentally acute and robustly athletic man who deteriorated into a morbidly obese, ill-tempered, paranoid, pain-wracked invalid. The sores on his legs—thought to have begun with a wound suffered in a 1536 jousting accident—did more than keep him from the dancing he had loved in his youth. They erupted and spread; they festered, often accompanied by fever. Eventually, they robbed him of the ability to walk.

Because Henry's many wives produced so few children healthy enough to survive infancy, it is natural for history buffs to wonder whether Henry's poor health also caused reproductive problems. Historian Susan Maclean Kybett has traced the syphilis rumor to nineteenth-century medical writer A. S. Currie, who with the aid of like-minded gynecologists argued that Catherine of Aragon's string of miscarriages and stillbirths indicated that Henry had infected her with syphilis. This line of thinking probably originated well before Currie gave it scientific credibility. It usually speculates that Henry and Catherine's daughter Mary I, who died childless at forty-two, suffered from congenital syphilis. Furthermore, it theorizes that Henry's son, Edward, the boy king who died before turning sixteen, was another congenital syphilitic and that Elizabeth I, the "Virgin Queen," may have avoided intimacy and marriage because of the disease she supposedly carried.

Syphilis is also suspected because of the times in which Henry lived. Medical historians disagree about how and when the spirochete bacterium *Treponema pallidum* arrived in Europe, but there is strong evidence that the subspecies of the bacterium that causes syphilis traveled from the island of Dominica, in the Caribbean Sea, to Spain aboard explorer Christopher Columbus's ships. Author Deborah Hayden, in her book *Pox: Genius, Madness, and the Mysteries of Syphilis*, notes that Columbus himself began to exhibit symptoms that could be attributed to syphilis on his second voyage to the Americas, in 1493. This subspecies, *T. pallidum pallidum*, either was new to Europeans or mutated into a tougher, faster-spreading strain of sexually transmitted disease about this time. Either way, the illness hit Southern Europe hard in the 1490s. Anecdotal reports say that sailors from Columbus's crews, at least some of whom had been intimate with native women taken from the west as slaves, first exhibited symptoms.

Shortly thereafter, in 1495, French king Charles VIII brought Spanish soldiers into his army, in preparation for invading Naples. By the end of the Naples campaign, thousands of people—soldiers, wives, camp followers, rape victims, and more—carried the infection. Syphilis became endemic (if not epidemic) across Europe and continued to spread, as little Henry Tudor, only four years old in 1495, grew into the bold, handsome teenager who inherited the English throne in 1509. Anthropologist Grace Q. Vicary has even suggested that the ornate padded codpieces worn by the noblemen of Henry's time grew so large not merely as an advertisement of masculine prowess but also to accommodate medical dressings for the treatment of chancres—the genital sores that indicate syphilis in its initial stage.

Author Hayden, whose book traces the progression of syphilis—confirmed or suspected—in a number of historical figures, does not go so far as to name Henry VIII as a syphilitic, but she calls it possible. Hayden explains that syphilis was especially difficult to diagnose before the advent of modern epidemiological tests. Its symptoms vary as the disease progresses, and they vary from individual to individual, often seeming to mimic the symptoms of other diseases—sores, rashes, swelling, and so on. The sores on Henry's legs may not have been typical of advanced syphilis, but what about the growth or deformity that developed on the right side of his nose? Syphilis notoriously attacks mucus membranes.

Another problem arises in lumping Elizabeth in with her half-brother Edward and half-sister Mary as infected with congenital syphilis. Elizabeth died at age sixty-nine, an advanced age for the time, and she enjoyed many decades of apparently quite robust health. Would that have been the case if she had been syphilitic?

The theory that Henry had syphilis, though impossible to prove (short of disinterring the king's bones), is well-enough entrenched that some Internet Web sites state it as fact. Still, even Hayden—who tends to see syphilis everywhere in history—admits to a problem in attributing Henry's ailments to the venereal disease: no surviving record suggests that the royal physicians prescribed mercury for the king. Mercury was the standard treatment for syphilis in Tudor England. Physicians bled Henry, bandaged his legs, and lanced his sores. They fed him potions and applied poultices containing ground pearls and lead, but they seem not to have used mercury. This would suggest that the king's doctors, at least, did not suspect that he had the pox.

The many stillbirths, miscarriages, and infant deaths in the royal household may indicate an overarching and contagious health problem, but modern readers need to remember that such tragedies were woefully common in the sixteenth century. About one in five babies died in the first year of life. At least a quarter of children failed to reach age ten. Nobody knew anything about microbes. Medicines and treatments often did more to harm than cure the patient.

Henry lived two hundred years before the Royal Navy surgeon James Lind would introduce the most basic sanitary procedures and the idea of preventive medicine. Perhaps also pertinent, Henry lived too early for Lind's most famous discovery: that eating citrus fruit can prevent and cure scurvy.

Historian Kybett is among those who have written that Henry and his wives and their children were probably severely malnourished. In a 1989 article in the British magazine *History Today*, Kybett made the case that all of Henry's symptoms—the sores on his legs and feet, the poor circulation, the swelling of his body and face, his rotting teeth, his bleeding gums and stinking breath, his deteriorating nose—even his mental and emotional decline—could have been advanced symptoms of scurvy. She found evidence for this in the fact that Henry's afflictions seemed to worsen in the late winter, roughly corresponding with Lent, a fasting season of the Catholic and English churches. As Easter brought an end to fasting and spring brought fresh foods—especially fruits and vegetables—to the table, the king seemed to get some relief from his sores and swellings. Kybett pointed out, too, that by choice, sixteenth-century English royals ate very little in the way of plant-based food, even when vegetables were most abundant. They considered the proper diet of the noble to be meat, fowl, meat, fish, and more meat. In England, most fruits had to be imported. Lemons and oranges were rare and expensive. Most nobles considered vegetables fit fare for peasants and other livestock, but not for themselves.

A long and severe vitamin C deficiency, Kybett argued, can manifest itself as bleeding gums, the loss of teeth, and sores on the feet and the legs. It can progress to extreme weakness and failure of the circulatory system, as well as deterioration of cartilage (the king's nose). Furthermore, malnourished people may experience intense cravings. Perhaps Henry ate so much, making himself obese, because he was trying to quench a craving with all the wrong foods. (Legend says that he particularly enjoyed eels cooked in animal fat.)

Other writers, notably novelist and Henry VIII enthusiast Tove Ford, who maintains Web pages devoted to the king and Tudor England, argue that swelling, throbbing veins, poor circulation, leg and foot ulcers, and necrosis of the toes all point to diabetes—perhaps juvenile (type 1) diabetes.

Historical novelist Nell Gavin has noted rightly that Henry could have suffered from both diabetes and scurvy. Perhaps he had diabetes, scurvy, gout, syphilis, and three or four other diseases nobody has thought of yet. His wives and children may have had various combinations of ailments as well. Given the time in which they lived and the descriptions of their various illnesses and deaths, it's likely that they did. There was no shortage of disease in Tudor England.

Edward VI's early death is generally attributed to tuberculosis (the same wasting sickness that killed his grandfather, Henry VII). Mary I has been thought to have died from cancer. If Elizabeth had sexual problems (and there's no hard evidence that she did), perhaps they were the result of a severe kidney infection that she suffered during Mary's reign.

The malnourishment theory, meanwhile, might fit particularly well with the feeble family birthrate. If Henry had scurvy, then perhaps his first wife, Catherine of Aragon, also was malnourished. It would follow that her pregnancies would be riskier and her children less robust. If Anne had eaten more parsnips and turnips, perhaps she would not have suffered a miscarriage in the summer of 1534. (She said it was the shock of hearing that Henry had been injured in a fall from his horse.) Perhaps a more nutritionally healthy Jane Seymour, wife number three, would not have succumbed to the infection she contracted giving birth to their son, Edward.

What about wives four through six? Henry found the fourth, Anne of Cleves, so unattractive that he never consummated the marriage and thus had an easy time getting it annulled. His fifth wife, Catherine Howard, was young and pretty and briefly rejuvenated the aging king, but by that time perhaps his failing health had made him impotent. (Catherine's extramarital affairs, which led to her beheading, might suggest that she was somewhat dissatisfied with the king's performance in the bedchamber.) Henry's final wife, Catherine Parr, remarried after Henry died in 1547 and promptly became pregnant, suggesting again that Henry was either impotent or infertile toward the end.

All of which, as the reader has probably already noted, adds up to nothing but speculation. Nobody knows and perhaps nobody will ever know exactly what ailed Henry VIII. His skeleton—or whatever remains of his body, interred in St. George's Chapel of Windsor Castle—may someday be subject to medical forensics. If so, investigators may or may not find signs of syphilis, scurvy, or another disease.

Short of skeletal proof, there seems little reason to brand Henry a syphilitic. His symptoms—especially the dramatic weight gain, poor circulation in the extremities, and sores that failed to heal—point more specifically to advanced diabetes. The scurvy hypothesis also seems far better supported, especially by the seasonal nature of the king's decline. Furthermore, even at his worst, Henry never exhibited the kind of mental breakdown that is consistent with tertiary stage syphilis. His mental state did deteriorate, but the deterioration manifested itself largely as paranoia, megalomania (not uncommon among autocrats), bad temper, and depression. If Henry had indeed contracted syphilis as a young man and if the disease had run its course, he is more likely to have experienced a complete personality change, which he did not. He probably would have, before his death, become so disoriented that he could not recognize where he was or those around him. Again, there's no evidence that it happened. He was cranky and stubborn—refusing to plan for his son Edward's imminent rule—until the end. He was Henry VIII until the end. Syphilis may conceivably have been part of who he was, but, without proof, it seems unlikely.

To investigate further:

Fraser, Antonia. *The Wives of Henry VIII*. New York: Vintage Books, 1994. A careful, well-researched account of the king's domestic life as focused on the women who married him. Readable, but not for those who haven't already familiarized themselves with the era and its manners.

Hayden, Deborah. *Pox: Genius, Madness, and the Mysteries of Syphilis*. New York: Basic Books, 2003. The author traces the history of the disease, focusing on famous sufferers.

Ives, Eric. *Anne Boleyn*. New York: Basil Blackwell, 1986. The author ties the rise and fall of Henry VIII's second wife to the larger political scene.

Scarisbrick, J. J. *Henry VIII*. Berkeley: University of California Press, 1969. The historian traces the life and reign of the monarch in a scholarly biography.

Starkey, David. ed. *Rivals in Power: Lives and Letters of the Great Tudor Dynasties*. New York: Grove Weidenfeld, 1990. Sixteenth-century monarchs are examined by means of their own words.

Weir, Alison. *Henry VIII: The King and His Court*. New York: Ballantine Books, 2000. A best-selling author's readable biography.

Wilson, Derek. *In the Lion's Court: Power, Ambition and Sudden Death in the Reign of Henry VIII*. New York: St. Martin's Press, 2002. This lively and entertaining examination underlines the dangers surrounding the Tudor king.

7

Is "Mary Mary" the Bloody English Queen?

Nursery rhymes provide us with a portal to the past. Many have been passed down through so many generations that their true origins and their meanings are lost to time. Most sound like nonsense, but there are hints in some that they might once have been intended as witty comments on political figures and current events. Just because a rhyme sounds as if it might once have mocked a monarch, however, doesn't necessarily mean that it did.

Theories abound about the original ideas behind some common children's verses. One popular and widely circulated notion about "Ring around the Rosie" is that it dates from the Black Death epidemic of the fourteenth century or from one of the plague's return visits to England over the following two hundred years. Adherents to this hypothesis think that "rosie" refers to ring-shaped rashes on bubonic plague victims. Folklorists dispute the idea, pointing out that no version of the rhyme with what might be taken as plague references appeared in print until long after the last epidemic scourged England.

Similar lines of thought about the rhyme "Mary Mary, Quite Contrary (How Does Your Garden Grow?)" speculate that it comments on the short, unhappy, sixteenth-century reign of Mary I of England. These notions also draw scholarly doubts. According to *The Oxford Dictionary of Nursery Rhymes*, "Mary Mary" first saw print in the eighteenth century. Researchers think it likely that if the rhyme was about Mary Tudor, the queen of England from 1553–1558, someone would have written down the verse earlier.

Yet oral traditions are oral. They don't necessarily appear on paper. If an eight-year-old girl from San Diego meets an eight-year-old girl from Boston, they're likely to compare notes—what their schools are like, what TV shows they like, whether they are on soccer teams, and whether they like or hate boys. Among the things they may find that they have in common is a fondness for a clapping game—a variation on pat-a-cake, often with complex clapping and slapping movements performed to a simple rhythm while the players chant a rhyming verse.

The first girl might start to teach her new friend how she plays the game in San Diego, and then the second girl will chime in with her slightly different Boston version. Not surprisingly, the words of the rhyme vary from place to place, player to player, but there are usually so many similarities that it's clear each child is part of the same little-girl tradition. Each is removed by a generation or a hundred generations from an earlier little girl—or big sister, mother, or babysitter—who taught two or more little girls an earlier version of the game.

An oral tradition is a living thing. The clapping game started who-knows-when in who-knows-what language. Perhaps it predated language. Perhaps it is as old as two children facing each other, each clapping her hands against the other's and giggling. Maybe it's as old as humankind. Folklorists spend their careers studying such phenomena, trying to pin down the roots and the meanings of rhymes and the patterns by which they spread from culture to culture. These scholars might be able to trace a song or a story as it traveled with soldiers or refugees in a particular war, as it crossed an ocean with traders. What researchers cannot do is travel back in time to hear the oral tradition when it actually began, as it spread. The resulting uncertainty leaves much room for speculation.

Fools (and smart amateurs, too) rush in where scholars fear to tread. Because nursery rhymes often make no literal sense, and because they are so catchy, people who have one stuck in memory have often thought about what it might once have meant and how it started. There is the strong temptation to find deep significance. Thus come theories such as bubonic plague "rosies" and a royal Mary Mary. They spring from the words, words such as:

> Mary Mary, quite contrary.
> How does your garden grow?
> With silver bells and cockleshells
> And pretty maids all in a row.

Mary Tudor was the elder of Henry VIII's two daughters, born in 1516 to his first wife, Catherine of Aragon. Mary did not start out contrary. The girl was considered extremely bright, talented, and well behaved. It must have been rather humiliating for her, though, when her father held out her little hand in offers of marriage to various European princes and kings in succession, using her as bait for an advantageous alliance. Perhaps even more embarrassing, none of those marriages happened.

When the princess was eleven, her father appealed to Pope Clement VII to annul his marriage to her mother. Henry claimed that the marriage was incestuous because Catherine had been his elder brother Arthur's widow before she married him. This was nonsense, of course. Henry wanted a male heir, as well as a younger, hotter wife (as explored in chapter 6).

Mary was certainly intelligent enough to know that what her father wanted to do would reduce her status from royal princess to bastard—the illegitimate issue of an illegitimate union. What happened from 1531 to 1533 was even worse. Henry, denied what he sought from the pope, separated from Catherine and married Anne Boleyn. Then, somewhat out of legal order (but he *was* the king), he got the archbishop of Canterbury to void his first marriage and got Parliament to declare the king supreme head of the English church, under no obligation to Rome. So there, Pope Clement.

As the new queen, Anne had no use for her predecessor's issue. She made sure that sixteen-year-old Mary never again saw her mother. Eliminated from the line of succession to the throne, Mary lost her palace in Wales and was forced to become a lady-in-waiting to her baby half-sister, Elizabeth. It must have stung.

In 1536, Henry accused Anne of cheating on him. Lacking a pre-nup, Anne exited the marriage (and this world) minus her head. Getting on with *his* life, Henry offered his daughter Mary a chance to regain his good graces—but only on the condition that she acknowledge him as supreme head of the English church. This was a tough thing for the young woman to do. Like her mother, she was a devout Catholic. Like her dad, she was stubborn. Finally, she gave in, but she always regretted it.

Another bitter pill for Mary came after the king died in 1547. Henry's successor was his little son (by his third wife), Edward, only nine years old when his father passed away. Although just a kid, Edward believed deeply in a Protestant version of Christianity. He didn't actually rule. That was done in his name by his uncle Edward Seymour and then by John Dudley. Both of them also leaned toward the Protestant camp and both worked to firm up the English Reformation. They wanted to finish the business Henry had started when he turned his back on Rome.

Dudley's policy involved strictly outlawing Catholic and other "nonconformist" worship. Princess Mary surely seethed.

Dudley, who got himself made Duke of Northumberland, liked being the power behind the throne. When it became clear in 1553 that young Edward VI was fatally ill, Dudley tried to block Mary from becoming the next ruler. The duke arranged for his son Guildford to marry Lady Jane Grey, the king's cousin. (It was a different time, granted, but even then, a kid growing up with the name "Guildford Dudley" must have been teased mercilessly.)

Now that the duke was Lady Jane's father-in-law, he persuaded the dying Edward to designate her as the next ruler, in place of Mary. This contradicted both Henry VIII's will and an act of Parliament. Dudley then actually got Lady Jane proclaimed queen, but this scam lasted only nine days. The English wouldn't stand for it. With the people's support, Mary Tudor rode into London and took her rightful place on the throne.

It would be understandable if she were royally ticked off, but, actually, Mary tried to keep her temper. Dudley senior, of course, had to be executed for treason, but the death sentence against Lady Jane and the younger Dudley was suspended—for a while. Then Lady Jane's father, who had been in on the whole "steal the throne" scheme, got involved in another plot against Mary, an armed rebellion. Heads rolled, literally. Jane and Guildford Dudley lost theirs, and things went downhill from there.

Mary was still a loyal Catholic, and she'd never been happy with England's break from the Roman church. She spent an enormous amount of energy trying to put English Christianity back the way it was before 1533. This was like trying to put the toothpaste back in the tube. It was both futile and messy.

She married her cousin Philip, the heir to the Spanish throne, and made him joint sovereign of England. Together they restored the Catholic creed and outlawed heresy against it.

During their reign, hundreds died for opposing the state and the church. Their government beheaded traitors and hanged rebels. Heretics, probably three hundred or so, were burned at the stake. Just about everybody who got caught openly opposing the queen and/or her faith died. To her people, the queen became "Bloody Mary," a name by which she is still remembered today.

Mary also joined Spain in an unpopular and unsuccessful war against France. Rather than gaining anything from the war, England lost its last territorial possession on the European continent, the strategically important port of Calais.

All of which establishes that Mary was contrary. Her faith was contrary to that of her predecessors and, by the time she ascended the throne, to that of the majority of English people. Her policies were contrary. She jerked the English church around into a U turn. In foreign policy she listened to her husband's family—the Hapsburgs of Spain, Austria, and the Holy Roman Empire—instead of to her English advisers.

Is it any wonder, then, that Mary I would be identified with Mary quite contrary? If the nursery rhyme originated during her rule, was it perhaps a form of political protest? When there was no freedom of speech, people often found roundabout ways to criticize or mock the government, ways that they could claim were harmless—a nonsense children's verse, for example. Yet for the Tudor queen to fit the verse, the other lines must also apply to her. What was her garden and why did it grow with silver bells and cockleshells?

In his book *Heavy Words Lightly Thrown*, British author Chris Roberts refers to the widespread belief that the silver bells in the rhyme represent thumbscrews, an instrument of torture associated with the Spanish Inquisition. As Mary was closely associated with Spain and Catholicism, and as her campaign against heretics in England employed torture, the connection may work. But was the term "silver bells" really ever a slang term for thumbscrews? And if so, why? The terrible machine—a miniature vise designed to crush a subject's thumb or finger, slowly and painfully—was neither bell-shaped nor silver-colored. It was generally made of black iron.

Roberts also says the cockleshells may be instruments of torture. The literal meaning of *cockleshell*, of course, is the shell of a bivalve mollusk called a cockle. It's a sea creature that's very much like a clam. Several Web sites commenting on the rhyme and its possible meanings claim that *cockleshell* was also the name of a device for squeezing a torture subject's genitals. Perhaps it was, but again, no authoritative source for that meaning of the word presents itself. Another suggested meaning for *cockleshell* is a shell-shaped iron mask used for torture. As with the previous suggested meaning, if such masks were called cockleshells, it was perhaps a private codeword known to only a few.

This theory then explains that "pretty maids all in a row" refers to an early version of the decapitation device that later, during the French Revolution, became known as the guillotine. The West Yorkshire town of Halifax acquired a machine with a weighted blade to cut off the heads of condemned lawbreakers sometime in the sixteenth century. In 1564, Scotland adopted a device based on the one used in Halifax. For reasons unknown, it was known in Edinburgh as "the maiden."

Bloody Mary Tudor was certainly associated with executions—but beheadings in London were still conducted with an ax, not with a mechanically aimed blade. Besides, most of Mary's executions were by hanging or fire. Furthermore, even if English executioners in places other than Halifax had used a "maiden," there certainly would never have been a row of them. Even the French Revolution never was reported to employ a row of guillotines.

If "pretty maids" references this kind of maiden, the Scottish maiden, then perhaps the verse would better be applied to the English sovereign's cousin, Mary, Queen of Scots (the subject of chapter 8). Mary, Queen of Scots, also was a Catholic ruler who contrarily clashed with Protestant subjects, but she was never associated with instruments of torture shaped like bells and shells. She did, however, have a retinue of four ladies-in-waiting, all of whom were also named Mary. Could they be the pretty maids of the verse?

Some theorists suggest that the silver bells represent the rituals and the wealth of the Catholic church—features of Catholicism that sixteenth-century Protestants objected to. Then the cockleshells might represent the shell-shaped badges that religious pilgrims wore on a traditional trek to Santiago de Compostela Cathedral in Spain, which was believed to be the burial place of the Apostle James. And the pretty maids? Well, perhaps they are Catholic nuns. The original, literal meaning of the word *maid* is "virgin," after all. But if the pretty maids are nuns, then wouldn't the "Mary" of the first line be the Virgin Mary, rather than a Catholic queen of England?

Other suggested meanings of the verse make the garden of the verse's second line into England itself and the "pretty maids" an ironic reference to a row of gravestones—clever, but not really convincing. And there is a school of thought that interprets the garden as the barren womb of Mary Tudor, who never "grew" herself a child to inherit her crown. In that argument, the "pretty maids" are a row of stillborns. This argument trips over the fact that Mary suffered not a series of stillbirths but a series of heartbreaking phantom pregnancies.

The problem with all such speculation is that it's just that, speculation. No one can know for sure who made up the rhyme and why. Without tying it to politics at all, one might imagine that the Mary of the title is simply a bride. Bells are a symbol associated with weddings—as in "wedding bells." Even today, the little bride and groom atop a wedding cake sometimes stand beneath a toy arch supporting a pair of silver bells. Cockleshells are a little more difficult to place in this context. One alternate meaning of cockleshell is a little boat—a boat just big enough for two, perhaps? Or perhaps it's relevant that another name for the shellfish called a cockle is "heart clam." Could the cockleshells be a reference to hearts? If it's not too great a stretch, perhaps they are hearts shedding their protective shells. Then again, *cockleshell* may have had a sexual reference lost to time.

A more pedestrian meaning for *cockleshell* might be a decorative bit of clothing. If the rhyme really did date to the sixteenth century, perhaps the cockleshell with its distinctive grooves is a pleated Elizabethan ruff, a fashionable collar of the time. Along this same line of reasoning, the pretty maids all in a row might be none other than bridesmaids.

There are also other ways to read the verse without endowing it with historical, political, or social significance beyond that of a simple bit of catchy doggerel. Maybe it's literally about a garden and all of the rest of the imagery—the bells, the shells, and the maids—are types of flowers. As tempting as it is to ascribe layers of significance to the seemingly innocuous, the effort is not always warranted. As Sigmund Freud supposedly said, "Sometimes a cigar is just a cigar."

To investigate further:

Bett, Henry. *Nursery Rhymes and Tales: Their Origin and History.* Detroit, Singing Tree Press, 1968. An enlightening examination of where well-known tales began and how they changed.

Burne, Charlotte Sophia. *Shropshire Folk-Lore: A Sheaf of Gleaning.* London: Trübner & Co., 1883. Tightly focused on folklore of this English region.

Delamar, Gloria T. *Mother Goose: From Nursery to Literature.* Jefferson, NC: McFarland & Co., 1987. Looks not just at rhymes but also at their influence.

Eckenstein, Lina. *Comparative Studies in Nursery Rhymes.* Detroit, MI: Singing Tree Press, 1969. A scholar's treatment finds import behind ditties.

Green, Percy B. *A History of Nursery Rhymes*. Detroit, MI: Singing Tree Press, 1968. Traces verses through various historical eras.

Opie, Iona, and Peter Opie. *The Oxford Dictionary of Nursery Rhymes*, 2nd edition. New York: Oxford University Press, 1997. The ultimate reference on the subject.

Roberts, Chris. *Heavy Words Lightly Thrown: The Reason behind the Rhyme*. New York: Gotham, 2005. Casually written, entertaining speculations on folklore origins.

Slack, Paul. *The Impact of the Plague in Tudor and Stuart England*. New York: Oxford University Press, 1990. Examines cultural and economic, as well as demographic, effects of the plague.

Varasdi, J. Allen. *Myth Information*. New York: Ballantine Books, 1996. Somewhat preachy in tone, the book corrects a wide range of popular misconceptions.

8

Did Mary, Queen of Scots, Murder Her Husband?

The murder of Henry Stewart, Lord Darnley, in the winter of 1567 resembles one of those mystery novels by Agatha Christie in which virtually everybody who knew the victim had good cause to wish him dead. Maybe this case was the template for such stories.

The details, however, would have been far too outlandish for the mannerly Dame Agatha. In a bizarre midnight episode, somebody apparently intercepted Darnley while he was fleeing a huge explosion that blasted his Edinburgh residence to pieces. That somebody then strangled the twenty-one-year-old king to death.

The title "king" suggests that Darnley ruled Scotland. This is not the case, but he was the queen's consort (that is, her husband), and his weirdly mysterious death stirred up enough trouble that it led to her losing her crown. Darnley had become king through marriage to his cousin Mary Stuart, Queen of

Scots, seventeen months before he died. The relationship gave him plenty of privilege but no kingly power, which was almost certainly a good thing. Handsome, charming, and reputedly a snazzy dancer, Darnley had won the beautiful queen's hand before she woke up to reality and smelled a rat—that is, the other side of Darnley's character. He drank often and to excess and whined incessantly about his lady love's refusal to grant him a legal authority called the Crown Matrimonial, which would have made him a coequal ruler with her.

Why did she balk? She was three years older than he and judged him still too immature. That's what she told him, anyway. But really, Mary was alarmed at what a spoiled brat her new husband was turning out to be. He was rude, greedy, self-indulgent, cruel, cowardly, unfaithful, promiscuous, bisexual, and very likely infected with syphilis. Even if he were legally qualified to be king, it's unlikely he would have risen to the challenge. When he was supposed to be by Mary's side in meetings of state, the lout was usually out riding his horse, sporting with friends, drinking, whoring, or doing whatever pleased him. Yet Darnley not only complained about not having royal power, he plotted to seize such power by virtually any means available.

In an act of monumental foolishness, Darnley joined a group of disgruntled lords in a plot to kill his wife's dear friend and personal secretary, David Rizzio, whom the lords thought exerted undue influence over Mary. The hateful Darnley even went so far as to insist that the murder be committed in Mary's presence, when she was seven months pregnant. (Historian Alison Weir has suggested that Darnley thought this might induce a miscarriage, so that the baby wouldn't precede him as a potential claimant to the throne.) As his erstwhile buddies murdered the secretary in a messy orgy of knife-thrusts, Darnley held tight to Mary to keep her from getting in the way or running for help.

After the murder, however, he lost his nerve, begged Mary for forgiveness, and turned against his co-conspirators. He tried to pin all the blame on them. Technically, after all, Darnley hadn't raised his dagger in the killing. Amazingly, Mary took him back, probably because she had little choice. By the standards of the time, she could have called for Darnley's head, but she didn't. She needed him alive and healthy, at least until her baby was born. Her enemies had spread ugly rumors that David Rizzio was the baby's father. That's unlikely, but Mary was counting on Darnley to put the rumors to rest by acknowledging the child as his own legitimate issue.

However useful he might still be, Darnley had shown himself to be a treacherous liability, and it is likely that Mary never again trusted him. Many contemporaries and generations of historians since have assumed that the queen was in on the king's murder, which occurred less than a year after Rizzio's. Mary did not exactly give the appearance of innocence when she married James Hepburn, the Earl of Bothwell, in May 1567—three months after Darnley's death. The Earl of Bothwell was a prime suspect in Darnley's murder. The hasty remarriage strengthened Mary's enemies' accusations against her and provided an excuse for them to remove her from the throne. Yet an inquiry conducted in her own time failed to convict her of wrongdoing, and serious doubts remain among some scholars today.

Mary had succeeded her father, James V, as Scotland's monarch when she was an infant. Reared in the court of Henri II of France (while regents ruled Scotland in her name), she had also been the queen consort of France during a brief teenage marriage to sickly King François II, who succeed Henri, his father, in 1559 and died the next year.

Mary's tumultuous and tragic life was shaped not just by her royal descent from the Stewart kings of England (certain branches of the family, including Mary's, changed the spelling to Stuart), but also by her royal descent from the first Tudor king of England, Henry VII, her great-grandfather. From the time she was a teenager, Mary had been told that she, not her cousin Elizabeth I, was the rightful wearer of the English crown. This was not technically correct. Mary's grandmother Margaret Tudor had renounced any claim to England's throne when she became the queen consort of Scotland. Yet in the eyes of Roman Catholics—including French and Spanish royalty— Henry VIII (Margaret's brother) never legitimately married Elizabeth's mother, Anne Boleyn, because he had never legitimately dissolved his first marriage. Thus, Elizabeth was illegitimate and, therefore, Mary (Henry VIII's grandniece) had a better claim than Elizabeth did to the throne in London.

Note the role of religion in this argument. Mary and Elizabeth lived in the century of the Protestant Reformation. Since 1517, when the German priest Martin Luther rebelled against the Roman Catholic Church, religious reform had rocked Europe, bringing about wars and rearranging the power structure of nations, especially in northern Europe. Catholics hated and feared Protestants, and vice versa.

While Mary was growing up Catholic in France, Protestantism had gained momentum in Scotland. In 1559, the fiery Calvinist preacher John Knox arrived in Edinburgh, the capital, and followers flocked to him. The young queen's return from France in 1561 put Knox and the Protestant nobles on their guard, while it gave hope to Catholics who sought to reestablish "the old religion." (Virtually nobody thought in terms of freedom of religion. Each European country was officially Christian, and each sanctioned only one brand of Christianity.)

There were also Catholic nobles who saw in Mary the potential not just for Scotland's return to the Roman fold, but also for England's reclamation. (The English church had broken away from Rome in 1534.) Those hopeful Catholics included influential lords in Scotland and England, as well as powerful Catholic rulers on the European continent, especially Pope Pius IV.

Among other potential successors to the English throne, one in particular had a claim virtually equal to Mary's. That was her husband, Darnley. Both were grandchildren of Margaret Tudor, although by two different husbands. Mary's father and Darnley's mother were half-siblings. Thus Darnley, who sometimes made a show of attending mass, also had the potential to gain backing as the great Catholic hope of Britain. He even made some attempts to win such support from France, Spain, and Rome.

The lords who murdered Rizzio, an Italian Catholic, were Protestants. By spreading rumors that Mary was having an affair with Rizzio, they duped Darnley into joining them. These lords actually wanted Darnley in on the deal because they planned to use him to wrest power away from his wife. They intended to terrorize or bully Mary into bestowing the Crown Matrimonial upon Darnley. Then they planned to put Scotland in the charge of the Protestant James Stewart, the Earl of Moray. There were two possible ways to do this: (1) Rule by making the weak-willed Darnley a puppet king, or (2) kill Darnley and put the Earl of Moray (a bastard son of James V, and thus Mary's half-brother) on the throne. For the first method, they would need to keep Mary out of the way, perhaps by imprisoning her. For the second, she would probably have to die along with Darnley.

The Earl of Bothwell, although a Protestant and at least as power-hungry as these other lords, was not in on the plot to kill Rizzio. A member of Mary's Privy Council, the Earl of Bothwell had a few years earlier run afoul of one of the most zealous Protestant lords, James Hamilton, the Earl of Arran, who had ruled Scotland as Mary's regent when she was a child in France. (Yes, this soap opera has too many characters to keep straight, but that's one reason why history is often so much stranger, and more confusing, than fiction.) The Earl of Arran suspected the Earl of Bothwell of trying to exert undue influence on the young queen. Aran imprisoned Bothwell in Edinburgh Castle, but Bothwell escaped. After adventures in England, France, and Denmark, he returned to Scotland to help the queen quell a 1565 rebellion led by the Earl of Moray.

The Earl of Bothwell established himself as someone the young queen could trust. That was important. Although Mary was older than her boy-husband, she was only twenty-three when Rizzio was killed. She was inexperienced, vulnerable, and justifiably suspicious of most of the nobles around her—not least the demonstrably untrustworthy Darnley. After Rizzio's murder, the Earl of Bothwell stuck by the queen, helped her to raise an army, and drove the lords responsible for Rizzio's death south, across the border into England.

Their enemies claimed that Mary and the Earl of Bothwell, who was about a decade older, were more than political allies during this time—that they carried on an adulterous affair that began not long after Rizzio's murder and well before Darnley's, and that they were enjoying secret trysts even during the peak of Mary's pregnancy. Most modern historians rather doubt this. For one thing, Mary was not in good health, either before or after the birth of her son James (later King James VI of Scotland and James I of England) on June 19, 1566.

Yet it is clear that the Earl of Bothwell—like virtually everybody else in this story—really was plotting to take control of the queen, just as the Earl of Arran had suspected. And it became clear that the Earl of Bothwell had been up to his neck in the plot to blow up Darnley.

In the bitter cold early morning of February 10, 1567, Darnley's half-dressed, strangled body lay in a walled orchard near a house that had just been blasted to rubble by a massive explosion. The body of William Taylor, his valet, also partly clad and strangled, lay a few feet away.

The exhausted townspeople who discovered the corpses at about 5 a.m. had spent the previous two or three hours searching through the smoking remains of the house, called the Old Provost's Lodging, which was part of a complex of buildings known as Kirk o'Field (after the church [kirk] of St. Mary in the Field) on what was then the south edge of Edinburgh. How the bodies got into the orchard is yet another royal mystery within this royal mystery. Who strangled them? Had they awakened at the sound of someone lighting a fuse and fled into the night? Did those who ignited the charge catch the king and his servant getting away and kill them? Is it possible that Darnley himself was in on a plot to blow up the house and make it look as if there had been an attempt on his life? If so, would he run half-naked into the frosty night to make his story more believable? And who would have caught and strangled him? It's certain that the two bodies had not been thrown clear by the blast because they were unmarked by powder, flame, or smoke.

The Old Provost's House had been Darnley's temporary residence upon his return to Edinburgh from Glasgow, where he had been recuperating from a terrible illness that had caused pustules to break out all over his body. Although some people at the time took the disease for smallpox and there were rumors of poisoning, it is just as likely that the sexually adventurous Darnley was suffering a second-stage attack of syphilis. During this period, Mary referred to Darnley as "pocky," a term she had used at other times to describe someone with syphilis.

For reasons both emotional and physical, Mary did not share Darnley's bed during his illness, but she had spent time with him and made a good show of reconciliation, even after the birth of their son. Was she sincere, or was she trying to keep the loose-cannon Darnley, who had recently promised to sail off to France, from hatching further plots against her? Mary had been responsible for bringing him back to Edinburgh and for establishing him at Kirk o'Field while he finished his convalescence. Mary's accusers say that this meant she set him up for murder.

Yet Mary spent the evening of February 9 with Darnley in the Old Provost's House. She departed less than three hours before the blast. This almost certainly means that the foundation and the cellar were being packed with gunpowder while the queen was upstairs. Does the fact that she left, rather than staying the night, mean that she knew what was going to happen? Or does the fact that she sat quietly with her ailing husband above an explosive charge confirm that she did *not* know about the plot?

Historians differ. Biographer Jenny Wormald, the author of *Mary, Queen of Scots: Politics, Passion and a Kingdom Lost*, finds the circumstantial evidence against the queen—especially her behavior after the murder—damning. Allison Weir, in *Mary, Queen of Scots, and the Murder of Lord Darnley*, finds it unlikely that the queen was one of the many conspirators against Darnley. Weir finds great significance in the fact that when Mary emerged from the house, on her way to make a brief appearance at a wedding reception, she remarked upon the "begrimed" face of her attendant Nicholas Hubert. Hubert (known by the nickname "Paris French") later admitted that he was among those packing the basement with gunpowder that night. The grime on his face had been black gunpowder. If Mary was in on the secret, why would she call attention to Hubert's dirty face?

James Douglas, the Earl of Morton and a leader of the Protestant faction, later said that the Earl of Bothwell had solicited his help in the plot against Darnley, assuring him that the queen had approved the plan. When the Earl of Morton asked for proof of her involvement, written in her own hand, the Earl of Bothwell could not supply it. Does that mean Mary was too smart to provide such evidence? Did the Earl of Bothwell lie? Did the Earl of Morton?

After Darnley's death, the queen seemed almost paralyzed. Despite urgent warnings from her few friends and even from fellow royals—including her cousin Elizabeth I and her former mother-in-law, Catherine de Medici of France—Mary did not arrest or prosecute anyone. She even failed to come up with a scapegoat. Instead, she suffered humiliation as a series of anonymous placards posted in Edinburgh accused her, along with the Earl of Bothwell, of the recent regicide.

So many people had hated Darnley. The killers of Rizzio, who had returned from exile, hated him for his disloyalty to them. The Earl of Moray hated him because he stood in the way of the crown. Everyone knew Darnley as a cruel coward, yet in the weeks after his murder he began to seem like a kind of martyr. The public wanted justice.

Finally, when the pressure became too great, the queen allowed the Earl of Bothwell to be tried for the crime. The proceeding was a sham, in which no witnesses were called and he was acquitted. Yet if Mary was protecting the Earl of Bothwell as a co-conspirator, why would he resort to kidnapping her?

That's just what he did on April 24. With a small party of attendants, Mary was returning to Edinburgh after a stay in Linlithgow (southeastern Scotland) when the Earl of Bothwell and an army intercepted her and escorted her to his castle at Dunbar. There, he held her captive, and, by most accounts of those at the castle, he raped her. Yet on May 15, she married him, apparently willingly. Then that summer, after a rare rebel alliance of Protestant and Catholic lords defeated Mary and the Earl of Bothwell's forces, she negotiated for the Earl of Bothwell's safety before agreeing to surrender her crown.

The dethroned Mary sought sanctuary with Elizabeth I in England. Elizabeth took her in (although they never actually met, even then), but more as a prisoner than as a guest. Five months later in York, English and Scottish nobles and officials gathered for an inquest into two questions. (1) Was Mary an accessory to Darnley's murder? (2) Did her Scottish subjects commit treason in rebelling against her?

The chief evidence presented against Mary (who was not allowed to attend) was excerpts from letters she had purportedly written to the Earl of Bothwell before the killing. Yet the letters (the originals are long lost) seemed to have been tampered with or even forged. At any rate, the verdict was "not proven" on both questions under consideration.

Mary Stuart, the former queen of Scots, spent the rest of her life—twenty years—in custody in England, where Catholic partisans continued to plot to put her on the throne in Elizabeth's place. Her complicity with such plotters eventually led to Elizabeth's signing a death warrant. Mary was beheaded on February 8, 1587.

To investigate further:

Cowan, Ian Borthwick. *The Enigma of Mary Stuart*. London: Gollancz, 1971. The author focuses on the many historical riddles concerning the queen's life and character.

Fraser, Antonia. *Mary, Queen of Scots*. London: Weidenfeld & Nicholson, 2003. The author brings the subject to life in the context of complex court intrigues.

Guy, John. *Queen of Scots: The True Life of Mary Stuart*. New York: Houghton Mifflin, 2004. A straightforward and accessible biography.

Mackay, James. *In the End Is My Beginning: A Life of Mary, Queen of Scots*. Edinburgh: Mainstream Publishing, 2000. The author focuses on Mary in relationship to Scottish, English, and French royal families and courts.

Plowden, Alison. *Two Queens in One Isle*. Brighton, Sussex, UK: Harvester Press, 1984. An examination of complex, distant, competitive relationship between the cousins Mary Stuart and Elizabeth Tudor.

Weir, Alison. *Mary, Queen of Scots, and the Murder of Lord Darnley*. New York: Ballantine, 2003. An excellent focus on the mysterious crime that led to Mary's strange exile.

Wormald, Jenny. *Mary, Queen of Scots: Politics, Passion and a Kingdom Lost*. New York: St. Martin's Press, 2001. Another examination of Edinburgh court intrigues that led to the queen's overthrow.

9

Did Elizabeth I Plot the Murder of a Famous Playwright?

The knifepoint struck Kit below his eyebrow, slicing through shallow flesh and skittering instantaneously down a quarter inch of blood-slicked bone into the socket. All the way through it plunged, slitting the eyelid, bisecting the eyeball, and disrupting the optic nerve and the ocular muscles on its way into the young man's brain.

Kit fell dead to the plank floor. It was late in the day and the sun hung low in the west. The candles were not yet lit. In the room's shadows the three other men present stood looking down at the body. There was silence except for the heaving breaths of Ingram Frizer, the man who had plunged the knife.

Much to the landlady's displeasure, the body had to lie there until the next day, June 1, 1593, when the coroner of Deptford, England, and his sixteen-man jury squeezed into the little, low-beamed space to view the undisturbed scene. Along with them came Frizer and the two witnesses—Nick Skeres and Robbie Poley.

The three men said that they had spent the day with the deceased, Christopher "Kit" Marlowe, who like them was from London, just three miles away. They came to the house in Deptford because the widow who owned it rented out rooms by the day, for meetings and such. She sold food and drink to her guests.

At the end of an afternoon of drinking, talking, eating, and more drinking, it came time to settle up with their hostess. Frizer, Skeres, and Poley worked out how much each of them owed as they completed a final game of backgammon. The three of them had been sharing a bench as they sat at a table against one wall. Kit, meanwhile, was splayed over a couch behind them, against the opposite wall. He had been dozing. Frizer called over his shoulder to Kit, telling him it was time for "the reckoning," their word for a bill. He told Kit what he owed, and Kit protested. He hadn't had more drinks than the rest of them, he said. They hadn't divided up the reckoning equally. They were cheating him.

Kit's companions told him to calm down, that they had figured out how much each of them fairly owed, and the amount they told him was his fair share. But Kit wouldn't calm down. Frizer was still sitting, facing the other way, toward the table. The room was warm and he had removed his doublet, exposing the large knife he always wore tucked in his belt at the small of his back.

Kit jumped up from the couch, grabbed the knife from Frizer's belt, and struck at the sitting man's head, inflicting a scalp wound. Suddenly bleeding, Frizer rose and turned, but he was not fast enough to avoid another slice across his pate. He managed to grab Kit's arm, and as he rose, he forced the knife up and back, turning it so that it plunged into his attacker's face.

In short, it was self-defense. Frizer had the bandaged head to prove it.

So the death of Christopher Marlowe—poet and playwright—has often been ascribed to "a tavern fight." Yet something has always seemed to be missing from the story. Questions linger. For one, who goes after a drinking companion with a knife over a simple thing like a bar bill? The conventional answer is that Kit Marlowe was notoriously hot-tempered and quick to fight, and that on this particular spring day in 1593 he was drunk beyond reason. Fair enough, but why couldn't three men subdue him? An angry drunk can be incredibly strong, as any modern police officer will testify, but so strong and quick that he could get the drop on three able men? So strong that the only way to stop him was to kill him? And for that matter, if the reckoning was such an issue, couldn't these men have asked the hostess for separate checks?

Note the weapon. In 1593 many men in London, if not most, carried knives. Marlowe was a brawler, a hothead. He probably had a blade on his person, too. Why didn't he reach for his own, instead of Frizer's? Now note the location of the wounds on Frizer's scalp. His scalp? Who attacks somebody with a knife on the top of the head? The slashes were more likely the result of close combat. Frizer threatened Marlowe. Marlowe grabbed Frizer's arm, deflecting the knife back and cutting Frizer's head. Then Frizer overpowered Marlowe and plunged the knife into his face.

Of course, people have died over grievances even more senseless than a few shillings, and it's true that all four men in the room had—at least, according to the survivors' account—been drinking for hours. Yet another fact about this killing is a bit more difficult to explain away. Two weeks after the fight, Queen Elizabeth I issued a pardon to Ingram Frizer. Case closed.

Wait. The queen? The head of state, the sovereign of the nation? She personally issued a pardon to a man who stabbed another man through the eye in a drunken bar fight? Something else was going on here.

First, these weren't just ordinary men. In the early 1590s, Marlowe was the most popular playwright in England. His plays—*Tamburlaine, The Jew of Malta, Doctor Faustus*—were the biggest things in Elizabethan entertainment since bear baiting. This was when Will Shakespeare's writing career was just getting started.

Although Marlowe was the son of a Canterbury shoemaker, he had gone to Cambridge and had a master's degree. But here's a curious thing about how he got that degree. The university at first turned him down for the M.A. His professors there were concerned about his frequent and unexplained absences. Then Cambridge received a letter from the queen's Privy Council, a group of lords who were Elizabeth's top advisers. It ordered the university officials to give Marlowe the degree, anyway, because "He hath of late done the Queen great service."

That great service may have been acting as a spy for her majesty. This is not as unlikely as it sounds. One reason that almost all the playwrights of the late sixteenth and early seventeenth centuries were university graduates (everybody but Shakespeare) is that university men weren't very well prepared to do much else in the world. Cambridge taught classic literature—the Greeks and the Romans. It taught rhetoric, just as the Catholic universities in France and Italy did. (Since at least the thirteenth century, Catholic scholars had found ways to bring pre-Christian "pagan" writers under the purview of Christianity, but that's a topic for another time.) England had stopped being Catholic almost sixty years before Marlowe got the knife in the eye. England had broken away from Rome back under the rule of Elizabeth's father, Henry VIII, but it was still turning out university men more or less on the old model.

So what else besides play writing were Cambridge men prepared to do? Many became Church of England clergy, but they were also rather well qualified to become Catholic priests—except that was illegal in England. This was, however, an era when Catholics from Spain, as well as Italy and France, recruited suitable young Englishmen for the priesthood. The tactic aimed at retaking Protestant England for the Roman church. The idea was to use the English priests as undercover agents in England, working to undermine Elizabeth's authority and to aid her enemies. This intelligence work tied in with plots by Catholic kings abroad and pro-Catholic English nobles at home to topple the Protestant Elizabeth and replace her with a Catholic monarch.

Elizabeth's government fought back by recruiting its own secret agents—university men like Marlowe. Until his death in 1590, Sir Francis Walsingham, the secretary of state and a member of the Privy Council, served as the queen's spymaster. His agents pretended to be Catholic sympathizers who were willing to take holy orders and work against Elizabeth. But actually, they were working *for* Elizabeth. That is, assuming the other side hadn't turned them into double agents.

Where did Marlowe fit into this complicated mess? Historians aren't sure, but it's thought that during his unexplained absences from Cambridge he was on secret missions to the European continent.

Moving on to Frizer, he worked as a sort of general assistant for Sir Thomas Walsingham, the nephew of Sir Francis Walsingham, the spy guy. Sir Thomas was also a patron of the arts. In particular, he was a supporter of the poet and playwright Christopher Marlowe.

As for the other two men who had been in the room—Skeres and Poley—they were seasoned spies. They had both been involved in an undercover operation that foiled a conspiracy to assassinate the queen. Poley had infiltrated the group that planned the hit. After the plot was broken up, Sir Francis put him in prison for two years to avoid blowing the spy's cover.

If Poley would spend two years in the Tower of London to avoid being fingered as a spy, couldn't Marlowe agree to disappear—that is, to fake his own death—for the same reason? Some people think Marlowe didn't die, that the whole thing was a charade and that he slipped away undetected to Italy. This fits nicely with theories that Marlowe actually wrote the plays attributed to William Shakespeare. An American, Calvin Hoffman, spent decades in the twentieth century trying to prove this. He thought he could find original Shakespeare manuscripts in the tomb of Sir Thomas, Marlowe's patron, and that the scripts would establish his case. Hoffman actually got the grave opened, but the papers weren't there.

Literary scholars think the similarities between Marlowe's plays and Shakespeare's aren't strong enough to show that the same person wrote them. In fact, they generally agree that the plays were written by two different dramatists. This doesn't mean that Marlowe couldn't have slipped away to Italy. He didn't have to write more plays there. For that matter, he could have written plays that no one ever produced or published. His friends and associates at the time, however, had no doubt that he was dead.

So if he died on that last day of May in 1593, and if it wasn't just a fight over the bill, what was it? Why kill Marlowe? And why would Elizabeth herself cover it up?

Could Marlowe have been killed because he was a heretic? Heresy was a serious business in 1593; it was considered an affront not just to religion, but to the queen herself. It was believed that God was the source of the monarch's authority. Heresy was such a grave offense that if convicted, a person could be put to death for uttering or writing statements judged to be heretical— that is, to deny God or mock the official creed of the English church. And not just put to death. The condemned was first hanged by the neck, but not in the "merciful" way where the neck snaps and brings quick death. No, this was a slow, painful hanging. Before the rope strangled the prisoner, executioners would cut him down and slit his belly open. They would pull his intestines out and burn them. The prisoner was supposed to be alive and conscious that this was happening to him (although he had probably gone into shock well before this time). Finally, they cut off his head and chopped the remaining body into four quarters.

Marlowe had a reputation for impiety, but then he had a generally scandalous reputation—for his brawling, his sexual affairs, his irreverent wit, and his wild partying. He had been accused of heresy, after authorities found papers, allegedly written by Marlowe, that denied the deity of Jesus. He was called before the Privy Council to answer the charge, yet they let him off with a warning. The councillors simply required that he check in with them regularly. It was like probation.

But what if the Privy Councillors were trying to use Marlowe as a spy again, an informant—not against Catholics but against, say, Sir Walter Raleigh, who had fallen out of Queen Elizabeth's favor and who was also suspected of heresy? Raleigh—the same Walter Raleigh known as an explorer and a navigator—enjoyed the kind of free-form philosophical discussions that could get an Elizabethan Englishman into trouble. He was also a friend of fellow intellectual Sir Thomas Walsingham, the patron of Marlowe and the employer of Frizer. Was Sir Thomas also in danger of being charged with heresy?

Sir Thomas no longer had his late uncle, Sir Francis the spymaster, to help him if he got into trouble. What if Sir Thomas discovered that he, his friend Raleigh, or both of them were the targets of an undercover sting? And what if he knew that Marlowe was the mole? Would he order Marlowe killed?

Maybe, but it's difficult, then, to account for Elizabeth's involvement. Why would she step in to protect Frizer, Sir Thomas's servant?

Here's another question: if Sir Francis had gone to such lengths to protect the cover of his agents, would the other members of the Privy Council know Marlowe had been a spy? Perhaps not. Maybe the only ones who knew any details were Elizabeth and her new secretary of state, Robert Cecil. What if Cecil, and maybe the queen herself, feared that a further investigation into Marlowe's alleged heresies would involve torture— as such investigations often did. Wouldn't they also worry that the playwright, under duress, might blurt out details of the secret spy network? Perhaps they engaged Skeres and Poley to organize an ambush. If that were the case, then Frizer, too, must have been a spy, which only stands to reason, as he was in the company of three other secret agents.

Perhaps it's relevant to this case that Skeres was also the servant of a powerful man. He worked for Robert Devereux, the Earl of Essex. Also a member of the Privy Council, the Earl of Essex was considered a great rival to Raleigh, whom he had succeeded as the queen's favorite. Might the Earl of Essex on his own have ordered his servant to arrange an ambush? If so, why? To score points with Elizabeth?

The ultimate question here is this: What did the queen know and when did she know it? If Elizabeth had not been in on planning the murder, why would she pardon Frizer? Could Marlowe have been murdered at the orders of Cecil, without the queen's knowledge?

No matter which of these people were complicit in the playwright's death, by themselves or in concert, and even if none of them was, the most probable reason for Elizabeth to pardon Frizer was simply that she could not risk having him put on trial. Whether Frizer was a spy for the queen or not, his companions certainly were. His victim probably was. Any further investigation almost certainly would have exposed state secrets that the queen could not allow to be exposed. Elizabeth needed this whole affair to be settled as simply, quickly, and quietly as possible. For that reason, Christopher Marlowe's violent death will always be swathed in mystery.

To investigate further:

Brimacombe, Peter. *All the Queen's Men: The World of Elizabeth I*. New York: St. Martin's Press, 2000. A fascinating portrait of the subtleties of court intrigues intertwined with dicey international relations.

Greenblatt, Stephen. *Will in the World: How Shakespeare Became Shakespeare*. New York: Norton, 2004. The author paints a vivid word-picture of Elizabethan England, with special attention to religious divisions that necessitated the queen's spy corps.

Hoffman, Calvin. *The Murder of the Man Who Was Shakespeare*. New York: Grosset & Dunlap, 1960. Hoffman argues that Marlowe survived the scuffle and lived to write Shakespeare's plays.

Honan, Park. *Christopher Marlowe: Poet and Spy*. New York: Oxford University Press, 2006. The author shows how a young man could be both an artist and an undercover operative in Elizabethan times.

Ingram, John H. *Christopher Marlowe and His Associates*. New York: Cooper Square, 1970. A look at Marlowe in the context of the figures, both literary and political, who peopled his world.

MacCaffrey, Wallace T. *Elizabeth I: War and Politics, 1588–1603*. Princeton, NJ: Princeton University Press, 1992. A scholarly examination of international pressures. Not for casual readers.

Nicholl, Charles. *The Reckoning: The Murder of Christopher Marlowe*. New York: Harcourt Brace, 1992. A vividly written telling of the story surrounding Marlowe's death.

Ogburn, Charlton. *The Mysterious William Shakespeare: The Myth and the Reality*. New York: Dodd, Mead, 1984. Mystery extends beyond the playwright, and the author's investigation sheds light on the culture and the politics of Elizabethan London.

Patterson, Benton Rain. *With the Heart of a King: Elizabeth I of England, Philip II of Spain, and the Fight for a Nation's Soul and Crown*. New York: St. Martin's Press, 2007. For the reader who wants a broader picture of the international enmity that shaped the queen's policies.

Riggs, David. *The World of Christopher Marlowe*. New York: Henry Holt, 2004. This thorough, fascinating examination of Marlowe the student, the poet, and the spy is crammed with information. This is for readers who have serious interest in the topic.

10

Who Was the Man in the Iron Mask?

Novelist Alexandre Dumas popularized him in print. Actors from Douglas Fairbanks to Leonardo DiCaprio have played him on film. In fictional retellings, the Man in the Iron Mask is unmasked, his identity revealed. He is the brother of the French king Louis XIV, his very existence a state secret.

The concept may be something like the truth, but nobody knows. The real-life mystery of an anonymous (or was he?) seventeenth-century political prisoner remains.

At this person's burial in 1703, he was listed as Marchioli, age about forty-five. French authorities routinely buried political prisoners under false names. The age seems highly unlikely, especially if Marchioli was the person—not a child—committed into the custody of prison warden Bénigne Dauvergne de Saint-Mars in 1669 and was the same prisoner who had moved from prison to prison with Saint-Mars over the decades since. As governor of the Fortress of Pignerol (then held by France, now

Pinerolo, Italy), Saint-Mars had charge of inmates who were of special interest to Louis XIV. For example, Saint-Mars's prisoner Nicholas Foquet had been Louis's finance minister and arguably the most powerful man in the king's court. Louis had ordered Foquet arrested and had taken a personal role in seeing that his three-year trial, on charges of embezzlement, ended in a conviction. Also interned at Pignerol, the hot-tempered Comte de Lauzun had been the captain of the royal bodyguard. Lauzun made the mistake of publicly denouncing the king's mistress during a dispute (involving love and money, of course).

Into this company came the masked man, preceded by instructions from the Marquis de Louvois, the war minister to the king. Louvois ordered jailer Saint-Mars to prepare a cell that was separated from any general corridor or outpost by more than one door so that nothing said in the cell could be overheard. "It is of the first importance that he is not allowed to tell what he knows to any living person," Louvois wrote. Saint-Mars was to treat the prisoner well and give him what he requested but was to threaten him with instant death if he spoke of anything beyond his immediate needs. Louvois added that those needs would not be great because the prisoner, whom he named as Eustache Dauger, was only a valet.

Yet rumors grew that the prisoner was someone else and something much more. Why was no one allowed to speak with him or see his face? Why was it said that Saint-Mars treated him with such deference and courtesy? Eyewitness accounts are unverifiable, but they describe the prisoner as tall with gray hair, dignified in bearing, and well mannered.

Only in legend, literature, and, of course, Hollywood is the famous mask made of iron. The most credible accounts describe headgear fashioned of black cloth, probably velvet. Yet the idea of a metal mask permanently locked to the head, a claustrophobe's nightmare, captured the imaginations of those who pondered the mystery. The great eighteenth-century writer

Voltaire, who heard about the prisoner during his own later imprisonment in the Bastille, described the mask as fashioned of steel with a spring mechanism to allow the prisoner to eat without removing it. Others imagined it as helmetlike, or just an iron face covering, perhaps like a hockey goalie's mask, that was secured with padlocked metal bands.

All of these versions of the mask may have arisen from the probably erroneous idea that the prisoner was required to cover his face at all times—an *iron*clad rule. It seems more likely that he wore only soft cloth over his head and face—a cowl like Batman's, without the bat ears—and that he could take it off when he was alone in his cell. The mask probably was required only when he appeared outside his cell or during the transfers from prison to prison during his life sentence.

But who was he? Just as nature abhors a vacuum, the human mind abhors an enigma. Was he Eustache Dauger, a valet? Some historians believe that Dauger had been a spy involved in top-secret negotiations between King Louis and England's Charles II. Perhaps he knew something so top secret that he could not be trusted with the information. But why hide his face? The name in the burial record, Marchioli, could have been a misspelling of Matthioli, the name of an Italian government minister who had negotiated a secret 1678 treaty with France and then betrayed Louis by leaking the terms. Louis did have Matthioli imprisoned at Pignerol, but many historians believe he died at another prison, Îles Sainte-Marguerite, in April 1694—not in the Bastille in 1712. Again, what need would Louis have to mask a man whose secret consisted purely of words—foreign intelligence data or the terms of a treaty?

Writers, raconteurs, historians, and mystery lovers have proposed many, many other identities—from royals to servants, French government ministers, a playwright, and even women. Most of these, upon consideration, have proved unlikely, if not impossible.

Some have suggested that the prisoner was Jean de Poquelin, better known by his stage name (and nom de plume) Molière. The playwright-actor had certainly made powerful enemies by satirizing French society's institutions, including the church and the university. He held nothing sacred and often violated the boundaries of discretion. Sharp comedies such as *Tartuffe*, which poked fun at religious hypocrisy, frequently landed him in trouble. Yet Molière's death in 1673, as well as his earlier frequent illnesses, were well-known. Why would the king—who was Molière's patron—fake a playwright's death just to lock him up? Besides, Molière was born in 1622. The sickly but outrageously outspoken genius seems an unlikely candidate to live into his eighties, the last thirty-some years in quiet, dignified solitude.

Another suggested identity is French general Vivien de Bulonde. Bulonde committed a terrible blunder at the Siege of Cuneo—a military conflict with the House of Savoy over land in the Italian Piedmont. The general ordered a hasty retreat, abandoning valuable munitions to the enemy and leaving French wounded and dead behind. According to another letter attributed to Louvois, Bulonde was to be imprisoned at Pignerol for this unspeakable breach of honor and was supposed to be masked when he was allowed out of his cell. Does that solve the mystery? No. The retreat in question did not take place until 1691. Bulonde was imprisoned indeed, but not secretly. He may have been masked (as a mark of shame, perhaps?), but he was not the Man in the Mask.

The names of British notables have been put forward, among them Richard Cromwell, the former lord protector of England, Scotland, and Ireland; the Duke of Monmouth, a pretender to the English crown; and Sir George Barclay, a fiercely Catholic Scot. All were part of the tumult and upheaval that roiled Britain through the seventeenth century. England experienced two civil wars (both in the 1640s), culminating with the beheading of a king (Charles I in 1649) and a short-lived republican government, the Commonwealth, from 1649 to 1660.

Richard Cromwell, the son of Puritan revolutionary leader Oliver, failed in his brief tenure as his father's successor. Internal conflicts, especially with the army, forced him to resign after less than a year as lord protector. He fled to Paris in 1660 to escape his debts. Even if there were a conceivable reason for Louis XIV to mask and jail the exile, Cromwell could not have been the mysterious prisoner buried in 1703. He later returned home and died in England in 1712.

After the collapse of the Commonwealth, the English restored their monarchy with Charles II, who died in 1685, leaving no direct heir. His brother, James II, became king. One of the late king's many illegitimate offspring—James Scott, the Duke of Monmouth—objected, proposing himself as a better successor than James. The Duke of Monmouth led a brief and futile rebellion. Convicted of treason, he was beheaded. Witnesses said that the executioner had to swing the ax many times to chop through James Scott's tough neck. Such a grisly detail makes it unlikely that, as some theorists have said, James II hadn't the heart to kill his own nephew and instead shipped the Duke of Monmouth across the Channel to Louis (who was Charles and James's cousin), where the pretender spent the rest of his life imprisoned as the Man in the Mask. Again, the dates don't correspond. The Duke of Monmouth's rebellion came too late.

James II survived that attempt to dethrone him, but as a Catholic monarch of an officially Protestant realm, he lost the support of churchmen and Parliament. In 1688, he also lost the backing of his army, and early the next year he was forced to surrender his crown to his Protestant daughter, Mary II, and her Dutch husband, William of Orange. This coup was called the Glorious Revolution.

Not everyone found it glorious. Both a Catholic and a be-
liever in the divine right of kings, Louis XIV had offered to come
to James's aid with French troops. (James II wisely decided it
would be disastrous to attack his own people with foreign soldiers.) Barclay, who conspired to assassinate William of Orange
so that James could retake England's throne, enjoyed French
backing. Why would Louis XIV imprison this conspirator? Because the plot failed? Unlikely. Besides, William took the English crown in 1689, well after the Man in the Mask began his
incarceration.

So it goes with many other candidates. The dates refuse to
match. No reasonable explanation for the mask presents itself.

The most popular theories that have been put forward cast a
close relative of Louis XIV, usually a brother, as the Man in the
Mask. These scenarios tend to hinge upon the curious circumstances of Louis's birth in 1638—or, rather, of his conception.
His mother, Anne of Austria, and her husband, Louis XIII, wed
in 1615 when they were both fourteen. Louis was not happy
with the arranged match. Forced to consummate the marriage
immediately so that it could not be annulled, the boy king felt
humiliated and avoided his teen queen for years. Later the couple, manipulated by courtiers, became close enough to bring
about more than one pregnancy and more than one miscarriage.
The king blamed the queen and remained estranged from her
for well over a decade. Then in 1638, just short of her thirty-
seventh birthday, Anne gave birth to the future Louis XIV. The
heir had been conceived, apparently, during a brief reconciliation, or so went the explanation.

One imaginative theory proposes that Anne delivered not a
son but a daughter. Under French law, only a male could wear
the crown. Louis (or perhaps his cunning minister, Cardinal
Richelieu) arranged for the daughter to be replaced with a baby
boy. This scenario requires the girl, presumably reared without
knowing her true parentage, to then somehow learn the secret

and threaten to reveal it. Yet no one who saw the Man in the Mask described anything womanly about the person's stature or bearing.

Another often-suggested candidate is Louis de Bourbon, the Comte de Vermandois. An illegitimate son of Louis XIV, Vermandois died in 1683, at age sixteen. Once again, the dates don't match. Furthermore, as in the cases of Molière and Monmouth, someone in authority would have had to stage Vermandois's death. But why? And why imprison the boy? Even if he were imprisoned for a reason that his father wanted to keep secret, why put the boy in a mask? Other kings had imprisoned and even executed their own kin—legal and bastard—for offenses real and imagined. Once more, why a mask?

Unless it was somehow symbolic, a badge of humiliation, the mask suggests that the prisoner would have easily been recognized and his face alone would have revealed a secret.

No photograph exists of the mysterious prisoner. The pioneers of photography, French inventors Nicéphore Niépce and Louis-Jacques-Mandé Daguerre, weren't born until about a century later. Printers, who could turn out 250 pages per hour on their hand-operated presses, used woodblocks and copper engravings to produce images. But newspapers were still in a rudimentary phase, and it is unlikely that many printed likenesses were widely recognizable. There was virtually no face that would be instantly recognized by those who had not seen it in person—none but the king's.

Louis's was the face of France, stamped upon coins and displayed in portraits hung in public buildings. The most enduring and seductive theory regarding the Man in the Mask is that he bore an unmistakable resemblance to that face. Thus, the identities suggested by Voltaire and (in fictional form) Dumas provide a logical solution. The Man in the Mask was a brother.

What if Louis XIV had not been Queen Anne's first child? What if, after repeated failures with the king, she had assumed that she couldn't have a baby? Imagine her surprise, then, if she found herself pregnant by someone else. In this scenario, she arranges to hide the first son. Then, knowing she can conceive, she lures the king to sleep with her so that they will produce another son, this one legitimate, this one the future king. The first son, his birth forever a secret, later becomes a problem and must be dealt with. Is the scenario possible? Maybe. This proposed series of events has a crucial fault in the unlikelihood that a half-brother of Louis XIV would so closely resemble the king that he would need to be masked.

Among Dumas's historical novels is a series called the D'Artagnan Romances, of which the most famous is *The Three Musketeers*. The series concludes with a very long book called *The Vicomte de Bragelonne*. In English translations it appears as three or even five volumes, each considered a novel in itself. The last, known as *The Man in the Iron Mask*, tells an imaginative tale in which it is the king's identical twin behind a face of polished metal.

Why hide a royal twin? In some unverified accounts of Louis XIV's birth, the arrival of the second boy gave rise to the question, who has preeminence, the first born or the first conceived? Today, it's well known that identical twins are conceived together as a single fertilized egg. It later divides into two embryos. The seventeenth-century French didn't know that. They thought that the second twin to be born was the first to have been conceived, and thus the senior. (Where they came up with such an idea is difficult to imagine.) To avoid a later conflict over the crown and a possible civil war, one of Anne's boys was taken away to be raised in ignorance of his true parentage. Little Louis, meanwhile, became the king upon his father's death in 1642. At some point, the secret twin would have seen a picture of the king, compared it to his own reflection, and begun to put *deux* plus *deux* together. After he came forward—perhaps to claim the crown, perhaps to blackmail his twin—the king and his ministers decided that the brother must be hidden away.

Mid-twentieth-century historian Hugh Ross Williamson offered yet another intriguing possibility, which he attributed to British politician Hugh Cecil, Lord Quickswood. In this imagining, the powerful Cardinal Richelieu decides that for the good of the monarchy, Louis XIII and Queen Anne must together produce a royal heir. He arranges a meeting between them at his own country house, assigning the couple to share a bedchamber. Yet Richelieu also strongly suspects that the sickly Louis XIII cannot sire a child. The cardinal convinces Anne that for the good of the country, or for her own good, or whatever, she must sleep with another man. Suppose that this other man, of good family but little wealth, is paid off handsomely to keep the secret and is urged to emigrate—to French Canada, perhaps. The problem arises when he returns decades later. He threatens to spill the beans—that the king is not legitimately the king. And to make matters worse, Louis XIV has grown up to look nothing like Louis XIII but instead is the living image of his biological papa. One look at the man from Canada and anyone would know he tells the truth. Thus, on goes the mask and the real father is sent into the care of M. Saint-Mars.

Williamson points out that correspondence relating to Saint-Mars's assignments after Pignerol refer to the masked prisoner, the one he was to take with him to his next posting, as "the old prisoner." It could be taken to mean the prisoner of long-standing, but it could also mean that the man was aged, old enough to be the king's dad.

There are problems here, too. For one, Richelieu and Anne were not allies in Louis XIV's court, but enemies. Around the time that the cunning cardinal might have been arranging stud service for the queen, he was busy humiliating her by exposing her secret, illegal, and potentially treasonous correspondence with her brother, Philip IV of Spain. France and Spain were at war. There is also the confusing fact that Louis and Anne had a second son, Philip, the Duke of Orleans, born in 1640. Was the first child somebody else's and the second really the king's?

Writer John Noone, in his book *The Man behind the Iron Mask*, offers yet another possibility. Noone focuses on the character of jailer Saint-Mars, an ambitious military careerist who often sought promotions during his long term as a prison governor and was frequently disappointed. Noone portrays Saint-Mars as a man eager to establish and maintain his own importance. He cites a prison memoir by René-Augustin Constantin de Renneville, another political prisoner whose stay in the Bastille overlapped that of the Man in the Mask. Renneville reported that the aged Saint-Mars was boastful and deceitful and that he made ridiculously exaggerated claims of past exploits and achievements.

Furthermore, Noone notes that financial records show that little money was spent to care for the man initially imprisoned as Dauger the valet—extremely little compared to that spent on prisoner Foquet, the once-powerful minister. Dauger was even assigned for a while to a job in the prison, as a valet to Foquet.

Who was "Eustache Dauger"? Noone thinks that he was none other than Eustache Dauger, a valet. Perhaps he was indeed a former diplomat or spy who knew too much, but he was not of the rank of Saint-Mars's other important prisoners. At Pignerol in the 1660s, Saint-Mars had come to think of himself as special, the keeper of a very elite class of convict. When he was assigned a mere valet—a valet with a powerful secret but still a valet—he decided to disguise the man's identity, to let it be believed that the Man in the Mask was a prisoner so important that he could be entrusted to none but the great Saint-Mars. Maybe the warden's superiors decided to humor him in this, to let him enjoy self-importance in lieu of a promotion.

Nearly four centuries before the mystery of the mask arose, a scholar known as William of Ockham (or Occam) wrote that "plurality should not be posited without necessity." This principle has come to be called the law of economy, or Occam's razor. It has been taken to mean that when choosing between competing explanations, one should choose the simplest. In the case of the Man in the Mask, the idea that historian Noone proposed seems simpler than the others. Behind the enigma of the Man in the Mask, there was only a man, a low-born man, a servant, a valet.

To investigate further:

Dumas, Alexandre père. *The Man in the Iron Mask*. New York: Penguin Classics, 2003. A novelist's imagining of the situation surrounding this prisoner has captured the imaginations of generations of readers.

Fraser, Antonia. *Love and Louis XIV: The Women in the Life of the Sun King*. New York: Nan A. Talese, 2006. An excellent popular historian, by looking at Louis XIV as a lover and a husband, illuminates the character of his court.

Kleinman, Ruth. *Anne of Austria: Queen of France*. Columbus: University of Ohio Press, 1987. A straightforward biography of Louis XIV's queen, with attention paid to the complexities of court life.

Levi, Anthony. *Cardinal Richelieu and the Making of France*. New York: Carroll & Graf, 2002. A fascinating examination of how a powerful churchman shaped the nation.

Lewis, W. H. *The Splendid Century: Life in the France of Louis XIV*. Long Grove, IL: Waveland Press, 1997. This cultural history helps the reader to grasp the era.

Macdonald, Roger. *The Man in the Iron Mask*. New York: Carroll & Graf, 2005. The author separates the novelist Dumas's characters from their real-life counterparts, in the process finding that a great deal of the drama had a basis in historical fact.

Mitford, Nancy. *The Sun King*. New York: Penguin, 1995. A scholarly yet highly readable biography of Louis XIV.

Noone, John. *The Man behind the Iron Mask*. New York: St. Martin's Press, 1988. The author presents his case that the prisoner's secrecy was never necessary but was a ploy by the prison governor to win attention for himself.

Williamson, Hugh Ross. *Who Was the Man in the Iron Mask?* New York: Penguin, 1974. This prolific mid-twentieth-century author examines the Mask legend, among other historical cases.

11

Did Catherine the Great Really Do . . . That?

"A lie can travel halfway around the world while the truth is putting on its shoes." Perhaps Mark Twain said that; perhaps he didn't. If he said it, he never wrote it down. Maybe whoever attributed the saying to Twain told a lie. Yet the great American novelist and humorist did tend to muse about the differences between truth and falsehood—often in tart witticisms, so the quote fits. It sounds like something Twain would have said, so people have no trouble believing that he did.

Regardless of who said it, the observation that a lie outdistances the truth is correct, especially if it's the right kind of lie. A juicy lie takes off like a jackrabbit and keeps going. If the story contains something that fascinates or disgusts, something so revolting or titillating that people can't get the lurid image out of their minds, the story will have staying power. The most enduring long-distance runners among falsehoods seem to be those that combine famous people with outré behavior. Even people who have never seen a silent movie believe that at a wild party in the 1920s, comedy star Fatty Arbuckle committed a lewd act that killed a young woman. Yet the truth is that he didn't do it.

So it is with Catherine the Great of Russia and the horse story. This lie, invented around the time of Catherine's death in 1796, gallops on more than two centuries later, spreading to new generations of the gullible. The truth comes panting behind, occasionally narrowing the distance but rarely pulling even.

Mention the czarina, the ruler of Russia from 1762 until she died, and somebody either asks about the horse story or thinks about it and decides it's too nasty to bring up in mixed company. Often, the horse story is the only thing that otherwise well-informed people know about Catherine the Great, except that she was Russian. (Actually, she wasn't. She was German.)

For those who *haven't* heard this lie, it goes as follows. Catherine II (the Great) enjoyed a vigorous sex life. As she aged, she found that her strong young lovers no longer satisfied her and she sought greater stimulation. Her death at age sixty-seven came when the harness that her servants were using to lower an aroused stallion onto the eager empress broke, causing the horse to fall and crush Catherine.

There. Once again, the lie has been repeated. Once again, someone is going to repeat the story without remembering that it is a lie. I repeat—it is a lie. It never happened. Catherine died, probably as the result of a stroke or an embolism, in her bed-chamber. An attendant found her unconscious on the floor of a closet adjoining her room, where she may have been using the chamber pot or washing. In other words, she had been getting ready for a routine day, not a wild bout of bestiality. Under the care of physicians and priests, she lingered until the next evening, November 6, 1796.

Rumors are notoriously difficult to track. In the twenty-first century, they often originate on the Internet, or they become e-mail or instant messages within hours of their inception. This makes it easier for a lie to spread and transform itself into an urban myth, but technology also allows those who study such things to get some kind of fix on *when* the story became contagious and maybe even *where*. A rumor from the late eighteenth century is considerably harder to trace. The horse story almost certainly arose as word of mouth and traveled rapidly that way for some time before anyone wrote it down.

Historians point out that the story circulated widely in France early in the nineteenth century and may even have arisen there. Yet it's highly probable that lurid rumors about Catherine were circulating through Russia during her long reign. Catherine, like any effective monarch, was no softy. She made enemies, even though she eschewed the most brutal cruelties inflicted by earlier Russian despots. She was not heartlessly insane, as were both her husband and immediate predecessor, Peter III, and her son and successor, Paul I. Early on, she even embraced the Enlightenment ideas of philosophers such as Rousseau, although she never found a practical way to apply such liberal idealism to the governing of Russia. Yet she was undeniably an autocrat and furthermore a usurper who had seized the throne from her incompetent husband. She was in no way descended from Russia's royal House of Romanov and thus lacked a hereditary claim to rule. Many Russians resented her.

Also, Catherine did value sexual companionship and made little effort to pretend that she did not. That's always an invitation to criticism, especially for a woman in power. She was not brazen about her liaisons, but she did take a series of lovers over the course of her reign. Most of these favorites, as they were called, were strong young military officers, and they got younger as she aged. Some historical-psychological diagnosticians have speculated that she was making up for lost time. The woman's one official marriage had been all but sexless.

Catherine began life as Sophie Friederike Auguste von Anhalt-Zerbst, an obscure but intellectually precocious princess from an obscure German principality (then a satellite state of Prussia, now part of Poland). Through interfamily politics, the girl's own strong personality and native intelligence, and a little luck, the Empress Elizabeth of Russia chose Sophie as a bride for her nephew Peter of Holstein-Gottorp. The childless Elizabeth, the youngest daughter of Peter the Great, had designated this nephew as heir to the Russian crown.

At age fifteen, Sophie converted from Lutheranism to the Russian Orthodox faith and was rechristened Catherine Alekseyevna. She became a grand duchess, and in 1745 she and Peter married. The luck that brought her to this station, however, was mixed. There may be no better description of Peter than this one from the 1911 *Encyclopedia Britannica*:

> Nature had made him mean, the smallpox had made him hideous, and his degraded habits made him loathsome. . . . He had the conviction that his princeship entitled him to disregard decency and the feelings of others. He planned brutal practical jokes, in which blows had always a share. His most manly taste did not rise above the kind of military interest which has been defined as corporal's mania, the passion for uniforms, pipeclay, buttons, the tricks of parade and the froth of discipline. He detested the Russians.

Beyond that, the boy drank to great excess. On their wedding night, Peter flopped into the nuptial bed beside Catherine so inebriated that he immediately passed out. When he was sober, their married life was hardly more satisfying. That is to say, it was not satisfying at all, to either partner. There would have been difficulties at any rate, because the sixteen-year-old bride, though very smart, still had not found out about the facts of life. When she asked her mother for an explanation, she got a smack on the side of the head. Peter was no help. He seemed both emotionally and physically unable to perform sexually.

This went on for years. By some accounts, Peter's physical problem was the result of a slight malformation of the foreskin of his penis. This seems to have been surgically corrected at a later date, after which the royal couple apparently engaged at least once in conventional intercourse, or Peter thought that they had. (He really did drink copiously.) At any rate, he accepted his wife's eldest child, Paul, born in 1754, as his son and heir.

By this time, however, Catherine had begun to take lovers—at the urging of Empress Elizabeth, who worried about the line of royal succession. Catherine, in her memoirs, let it be understood that none of her three children was her husband's.

After Elizabeth died in 1762, Peter ascended to the throne as Peter III. His short reign was a disaster. Contrary to his aunt's long-established foreign policy, Peter revered the state of Prussia, an enemy in the Seven Years' War. Upon taking power, he immediately pulled Russia's forces—on the brink of victory—out of the war. This and other capricious decisions enraged the military. Peter, meanwhile, alienated the Russian church by trying to force upon it the Lutheran practices of his native Holstein.

The new czar, foolish to the point of madness, had never bothered to build a political framework of allies. Without friends in the bureaucracy, the army, or the clergy, he could not rule. While Catherine's husband had been spewing his hatred of all things Russian, Catherine had conscientiously transformed herself into a Russian. She mastered the language, the culture, and the politics. Six months into Peter's reign, it was she who enjoyed the support of the military, the aristocracy, and the public.

On June 28, 1762, she and her lover, Grigory Grigoryevich Orlov, the leader of the anti-Peter conspiracy, rode into St.

Petersburg at the head of a column of regiments that were loyal to her. There she was proclaimed empress. Orlov's brother, the army officer Alexy, went to Peter's country palace and compelled the czar to abdicate. Eight days later, someone among the new czarina's supporters—possibly, Alexy Orlov himself—killed Peter. Catherine probably did not order the assassination, but many among the public blamed her.

Grigory Orlov had not been Catherine's first lover, and he would not be her last, not even close. Over the following three decades, the empress practiced serial monogamy—staying with one lover, usually for a matter of years, and then moving on to another. It is widely thought that she secretly married the most famous of these paramours, Grigori Alexandrovich Potemkin.

Catherine left each lover, usually on good terms, handing out titles and estates as consolation prizes when she dumped a boy toy. In Potemkin's case, she recognized his leadership talent and intellectual abilities, which led her to install him in some of the government's most important jobs. He advanced from the rank of second lieutenant to become a prince of Russia and remained one of the most powerful officials in Catherine's empire years after she no longer shared her bed with him.

In her later life, the empress seemed somewhat less interested in emotional and intellectual companionship in her paramours. At any rate, the men got younger and arguably hunkier. Legends grew up over this behavior. It was said that Potemkin himself procured the lovers from among his regimental officers and that a favorite lady in waiting, a countess, gave each candidate a "test drive," as it were, to see if he was up to Catherine's standards.

Some of this may be true or partially true. "In all lies there is wheat among the chaff," as Mark Twain wrote. Rumors of Catherine's need for a man in her bed surely spread and no doubt became exaggerated, perhaps even wildly exaggerated. Without doubt, she was the subject of dirty jokes. What ruler isn't?

Another bit of wheat among the chaff may be Catherine's love of horses—no, not a perverted love, but the kind that a horsewoman feels toward her steed. She was, at any rate, an avid rider. During the long, frustrating years of her marriage to Peter, she spent much time riding. And there was a detail about her riding that surely raised a few eyebrows, perhaps also sparking a rumor or two. Catherine rode astride the horse. This was considered unladylike and immodest in an age of side-saddle propriety. It was even considered dangerous for a woman to straddle a saddle. The Empress Elizabeth worried that Catherine would render herself unable to have children.

Is it possible that Catherine, when she was a young grand duchess trapped in a marriage without either love or sex, found some physical gratification in horseback riding? Sure, it is. Furthermore, it would be surprising if the way she rode didn't spark a rude comment or two.

Rude comments, unless they are extraordinarily clever, fall away over time. They are forgotten. The obscene myth about Catherine's death is much more than that, and it stubbornly refuses to fall away.

The best explanation for the horse story is that it began with Catherine herself. Not that the empress did anything like what the story relates. Nor did she make up the story; this is not an attempt to blame the victim. She merely liked horses and sex. She was an autocrat, and so she was indulged. She could order people to do whatever pleased her. With a male companion, she had led a coup against her husband and czar. Afterward, she took little trouble to pretend that she, as a widow, led a chaste existence. Thus, whoever invented the horse story concocted a perfect mix of rumor ingredients. The story, as outrageous as it was, and still is, had elements of Catherine about it. It's likely that a minor Russian noble or a French revolutionary would have heard that story and thought that it sounded exactly like something the randy old empress would have done—all the while ignoring an inner b.s. detector that said the tale was a crock. The hearer may not have hesitated to tell it to the next person—whether in Russia, France, Germany, or America—and that person might have jumped at the chance to repeat the tale. Thereby, the lie would have been off upon its travels.

Catherine seemed not to mind being known as healthily lusty. She probably took a certain pride in her string of lovers, perhaps even to the point that she pretended to be a bit more wanton than she really was. From her memoirs, it seems clear that she wanted all to know that the father of the Emperor Paul, her son, was her first lover, the tall, handsome Serge Saltykov. Yet the stubby Paul looked nothing like Saltykov. If he resembled anyone, it was Peter III, still alive and legally wed to Catherine when the baby was born. As an adult, Paul also shared the late czar's personal quirks, including a juvenile streak of cruelty and a strange affection for everything Prussian. Also like Peter III, he became a capricious tyrant who made enemies of his own officials. Could Catherine have done something so conventional as bearing her husband's legitimate heir? Who would believe it?

To investigate further:

Alexander, John T. *Catherine the Great: Life and Legend*. New York: Oxford University Press, 1989. A comprehensive biography of the empress, with much background on the context of her time.

De Madariaga, Isabel. *Catherine the Great: A Short History*. New Haven, CT: Yale University Press, 1990. This accessibly concise book simplifies the story but does not distort it.

Erikson, Carolly. *Great Catherine*. New York: St. Martin's Press, 1994. The biographer skillfully depicts the empress's extraordinary strength of character.

Farquhar, Michael. *A Treasury of Royal Scandals: the Shocking True Stories of History's Wickedest, Weirdest, Most Wanton Kings, Queens, Tsars, Popes, and Emperors*. New York: Penguin, 2001. The author skims through royal misbehaviors, including Catherine's sex life.

Montefiore, Simon Sebag. *Potemkin: Catherine the Great's Imperial Partner*. New York: Vintage Books, 2005. A biography of the powerful prince who many believe was the empress's secret husband.

Rounding, Virginia. *Catherine the Great: Love, Sex and Power*. New York: St. Martin's Press, 2007. This well-written and thorough biography integrates the empress's public and private personas.

Shaw, Karl. *Royal Babylon: The Shocking History of European Royalty*. New York: Broadway Books, 1999. Aiming for amused titillation, this book includes Catherine among the world's lusty royals.

12

What Made George III Insane?

lmost 150 years after King George II died in 1820, modern medicine began to make sense of the mysterious ailment that, sporadically and cumulatively, especially over the last two decades of his long reign, rendered Britain's monarch tragically insane. The operative word is *began*.

George III's dementia had a physical cause. Many painful symptoms both preceded and accompanied it. Doctors of the time knew that mental and physical illnesses often are linked, but they knew little about the actual causes of disease. They had not come very far beyond the Medieval idea of four cardinal humors—blood, phlegm, choler, and melancholy—that governed both health and personality. When researchers Ida MacAlpine and Richard Hunter announced, in the 1960s, that the mad king had suffered from a form of porphyria, they named a specific mechanism that could have caused his physical torment—abdominal pain, pain in the limbs, constipation, skin rashes, and more—and that could have simultaneously scrambled his ability to think and to perceive the reality around him.

The proposal, put forward by the mother-son team of medical-historical scholars in their 1969 book *George III and the Mad-Business*, makes sense, although it cannot be proved. Yet if George's complaint was a kind of porphyria, there is more to the medical mystery than simply naming the ailment. Porphyrias rarely exhibit such extreme symptoms as those the king suffered. The porphyria theory, shared by many historians and biographers, is built on compiling symptoms among the king's family (his children and siblings also exhibited unexplained symptoms) and his ancestors all the way back to Mary, Queen of Scots. In most cases, especially in previous generations, the symptoms were mild—sensitivity to the sun, rashes, occasional bouts of sharp pain in the abdomen, chronic constipation, vomiting, and so on. But no one before him had gone insane; few had suffered as he did. Why was his case so terrible? And why would a genetic disease, presumably present since conception, lie dormant until George was fifty before it began to trouble him so?

Americans like to think of George III, who was king during the American Revolution, as a tyrant, a greedy despot who taxed the colonists without giving them a say in the matter and who was driven bonkers by his failure to hang onto the colonies. Not so, say his defenders. The ruler was neither a tyrant nor a dolt. In reality, he was probably much like the semisympathetic and complicated character played by actor Nigel Hawthorne in the 1994 film *The Madness of King George*. At any rate, the king's madness stemmed from disease, not merely from brooding over a lost war, lost lands, or lost tax revenues.

Born in 1739, the king was the grandson of George II. Georges I and II had been born and reared in Hanover, a state within the Holy Roman Empire (now part of Germany). They had come to the throne through their descent from the Electress Sophia of Hanover, a granddaughter of James I. Neither of these

German kings had much cared for England, its customs, or its people. George I never bothered to learn the language, and George II spoke it with a heavy accent. George III, by contrast, was born in London, considered himself British, and tried very hard to heal the rift between British sovereign and British subjects that had widened during the reigns of his two immediate predecessors.

It appeared that George III had to try hard in order to succeed at anything. When he was a boy, his tutors found him difficult, nearly hopeless, to teach. He was oddly lethargic, as if depressed. He had a great deal of trouble paying attention. He was very slow to learn to read. In an era when elegant handwriting was considered a hallmark of an educated man, the prince produced an execrable scrawl. His writing as a young adult was little better than that of a small boy. In later centuries, young George might have been called slow or a late bloomer. Today he would probably receive the label of learning disabled or developmentally delayed or both. At the time—especially after his father died in 1651, making George heir to the crown—contemporaries worried that their future king was just plain stupid.

It turned out that he was not. Young George found a mentor in his parents' friend John Stuart, the Earl of Bute, who encouraged an interest in botany and impressed upon the prince the importance of preparation and self-discipline in facing his coming responsibilities. When George became king in 1660, he made Bute his chief adviser. In 1662 the king elevated Bute to de facto prime minister, a role for which the Scottish nobleman was ill-suited. That was one of many mistakes that the new king made. George was naive about politics, but he applied himself diligently to state business, insisting on reading every word of every bit of legislation that crossed his desk. He labored to understand the workings of Parliament. He tried to learn from his errors. Sometimes he even succeeded. When his reliance on

Bute proved a hindrance and led to embarrassment for the king, he dismissed his mentor and moved on.

In his personal life, George exhibited traits of modesty and parsimony. He enjoyed walking and riding, usually without a retinue. Dressed plainly, he frequently hailed commoners he met upon the road and conversed with them. Often, they had no idea of the identity of the eccentric gentleman who punctuated his talk with the exclamations "What, what!" and "Hey, hey!" The king loved farming and was happy to talk about that subject until his listeners wanted to plant their heads in freshly plowed soil. One of his nicknames was Farmer George. Yet he also enjoyed music and literature. He collected books, to such an extent that the British Museum library was founded upon the king's collection. Beyond that, he collected drawings and coins, as well as other items that displayed the artistry and the fine craftsmanship he admired.

George and his queen, Charlotte of Mecklenburg, lived simply. By the standards of royalty, their tastes were austere. Their diet of mutton, potatoes, and brussels sprouts rarely varied. The king worried about his weight and tried to eat sparingly. They drank little wine, and what they drank was inexpensive and reputedly awful. They seldom entertained or ventured out in the evening. They liked quiet nights at home and early bedtimes—night after night after night for decades on end. Of their fifteen children, fourteen lived to adulthood, and, to varying extents, all found court life stultifying. It was especially hard on the six girls because their overprotective parents refused to let them marry. For a well-bred English girl, marriage was nearly the only way out from under her parents' roof, so the princesses could not escape even as adults. The eight boys, including future kings George IV and William IV, got their own lodgings at the first opportunity.

Although the king's tastes were simple, the times were not. In addition to the political intrigues of Parliament, George III faced many challenges abroad and at home. The same economic pressures and evolving social philosophies that led to the American and the French revolutions were at work in other parts of George's realm, not least at home in England. John Wilkes, a radically liberal journalist and a member of Parliament, attacked the young king in print throughout the 1660s, at one point inciting riots in the streets. Catholics—long banned from voting, inheriting land, or serving in the British military—pushed for emancipation, against strong opposition from the majority of English citizens, as well as from the king. The Catholic Relief Act of 1778 led to a violent Protestant backlash in London in 1780. At the same time, the Irish agitated for independence, a movement that would result in a 1798 armed uprising. The Industrial Revolution was also under way, intensifying class and economic distinctions and breeding discontent. Manual craftsmen rioted against the machines that took their livelihoods away. Peasants also lost their means of sustenance as wealthy private owners enclosed formerly public lands, which had traditionally been used by the landless to graze livestock and for family farm plots. Country people flocked to cities in search of jobs. Slums sprang up. From 1793 onward, Great Britain was at war with revolutionary France.

Against this background, George III persevered, if not with grace, then with a stolid sense of duty. When able, he worked hard. His reign officially lasted almost sixty years—the longest of any British monarch except for that of his granddaughter Victoria, who ruled from June 1837 to January 1901. During the last years of George's reign, however, he could not work. He could rarely do more than gibber. After much debate, Parliament in 1811 appointed the Prince of Wales (the future George IV) as regent (a sort of pinch-hitter for the king).

In examining the illness, some historians have started in 1788, when George III suffered an attack of biliousness (liver trouble) followed by more severe symptoms, among them a temporary mental derangement that presaged the later, longer, deeper dementia. The tendency to pinpoint the beginning of his madness to this episode has led to the much-cited, but erroneous, observation that porphyria (if that is what it was) did not attack George III until he was fifty. Yet it almost certainly troubled him much earlier.

The king suffered unexplained periods of ill health from the first few years of his reign. He spent the first six months of 1762 unwell. His symptoms included a rapid pulse, insomnia, and a fever. An illness that struck him in 1765 brought sharp pains in his chest. He suffered symptoms again the next year. George was not, however, a sickly sort. That is, between recurrences he bounced back and enjoyed vigorous health. He relished regular exercise and kept fit.

Because porphyria spreads genetically, it is a lifelong condition. George's form of the disease appears to have been acute intermittent porphyria. Passed on as a dominant genetic trait, it is a deficiency of an enzyme that is essential in producing heme. Heme is the dark-red biochemical component of the protein hemoglobin, which carries oxygen in the blood. Symptoms of this disorder arise from insufficient heme, which binds to oxygen, and from the buildup of chemical precursors to heme in the blood. In the presence of the enzyme, called porphobilinogen deaminase, these chemicals join to become heme. Without enough of the enzyme, some of the chemical precursors have nowhere to go and nothing to cause but trouble. The king's type of porphyria falls under the category of hepatic porphyrias, which means that the initial metabolic hitch takes place in the liver. It can be almost entirely asymptomatic. When it is not, the symptoms come on in response to any of a number of triggers, including certain medicines and hormonal changes. In women, pregnancy can trigger an attack.

The disease is inconsistent, striking each individual a bit differently. Its most common symptoms include sharp abdominal pain, chronic constipation, pains in the extremities, weakness or paralysis, nasty skin rashes, and sensitivity to light. The give-away to diagnosticians is that the patient's urine turns dark, often deep red or purple. King George's physicians described his urine as port-wine colored, brown, red, and also, alarmingly, blue.

The worst symptoms of acute intermittent porphyria are the effects upon the nervous system, especially the brain. Patients can become confused, disoriented, agitated, hyperactive, and hysterical. They can experience hallucinations. George III, unfortunately for both him and Britain, suffered virtually every symptom. By the time he died—blind, deaf, and unaware of the world around him—he had been beyond hope for almost a decade. From the 1788 attack onward, his episodes of dementia caused him to swear obscene oaths and make inappropriate ad-vances toward women, denunciations of Queen Charlotte (who did not deserve them), and professions of love and lust for a respectable acquaintance, Elizabeth Spencer. He was so unlike his usual self that he sometimes seemed the opposite of the carefully moral and self-disciplined George—as if he were another being, the anti-George. One exceptionally lucid day in 1817, the elderly king announced that he would have a new suit made, "And I will have it black in memory of George III, for he was a good man."

Although porphyria was common among English royals from the seventeenth century onward, no previous family mem-ber had suffered anything like such an extreme case. Most men with porphyria don't even exhibit symptoms. What made poor George III so different from his direct ancestor James I, also a porphyria sufferer but one who hardly showed it?

In 2004, British researchers found more clues, starting with an analysis of George's hair, a tuft of which had been preserved in an envelope. To their surprise, it contained three hundred times the toxic level of the poison arsenic. Where did all that arsenic come from? Arsenic was a component in many commercial products in the eighteenth and early nineteenth centuries. It could be found in wig powders and face creams, but not in high concentrations. How did George absorb so much of the poison? And what was the effect of chronic, long-term arsenic poisoning—for nothing else could explain the huge concentration in the hair sample—on a man with a hereditary metabolic disease?

It turns out that one of the long list of things that can trigger an attack of acute intermittent porphyria—as confirmed by modern case studies—is exposure to arsenic. How much arsenic? Like so many other things about this illness, the amount varies. Where did the poisonous substance come from? According to notes from the king's doctors, preserved in a royal archive, the king when ill was dosed several times a day with Dr. James's Powder, a preparation made of the metallic element antimony. As a medicine, antimony can help to induce nausea—perhaps to ease the king's "excess of bile"—and it was also prescribed to loosen congestion in the chest. Generally derived from the mineral stibnite, which in turn can be harvested from the metamorphic rock gneiss, antimony is often mixed with another mineral element, arsenic. It is almost certain that the antimony administered to George was contaminated.

That gradual poisoning, which built up the amount of arsenic in his system over years and decades, probably accounts for how terrible the king's illness eventually became. It does not, however, explain what initially brought on the illness. Clearly, the health problems reported in the 1760s were early attacks. What triggered them?

The answer can be found on the "Learning about Porphyria" Web site of the National Human Genome Research Institute. Among the porphyria triggers listed are physical and emotional stresses. When George began to experience attacks, he was a young king, still under twenty-five. He took the throne in the middle of the Seven Years' War, bringing with him an ill-equipped adviser in Lord Bute. That would be a stressful situation for anyone, but it may have been incredibly stressful for this particular young man. He had struggled mightily to learn to read and had barely been able to write at age twenty, not long before he became king. Descriptions of his youth make it clear that he was handicapped by some sort of developmental delay. Like many people with learning disabilities—ranging from attention deficit disorder (which he may also have had) to dyslexia—he probably worked incredibly hard to hide and compensate for his weakness. His later extreme fondness for quiet evenings and solitary rides could be further evidence, because people who must exert themselves to function in work and social situations tend to require more dedicated downtime than others do. Because they make such an effort to present an outward image of competency and normalcy, they must regularly turn away from the outside world, giving themselves a chance to recharge their emotional and mental batteries.

When George became king and suddenly faced savage attacks by Wilkes, he realized the inadequacies of Bute, the man he had depended on. Being king must have put him under enormous pressure. He was a slow learner who faced a steep learning curve, with all eyes upon him. He had a strong sense of responsibility, making it harder for him to shrug off his mistakes.

His attacks of porphyria in later decades may also be linked to periods of extreme stress. His 1788 attack, for example, came at a time when the clean-living, somewhat priggish king was extremely upset over his sons' fondness for women and strong drink. The Prince of Wales, especially, had caused his father grief by a supposedly "secret" marriage to a Catholic widow. And there was that business about the American colonies. George reportedly took the loss hard, even talking about it during his bouts of madness.

Finally, the king may have deprived himself of a common defense against porphyria. Doctors have found that a high-carbohydrate diet can ease symptoms and even forestall attacks. In 2005, researchers at the Dana-Farber Cancer Institute in Boston identified the molecular process within the liver that brings about porphyria. In doing so, they confirmed something that doctors and sufferers had long noted—that carbohydrates can stave off attacks and that fasting can trigger them. Some porphyria sufferers may even crave large amounts of carbs. Such cravings may have had something to do with the progressive obesity of Queen Victoria.

George, however, worried about the family tendency to grow fat. Portraits from his prime show him as full-faced and filling out his waistcoat, but he fought weight gain by sticking to plain food—mostly mutton and vegetables. During his health crisis of 1788, one of his many doctors made the comment—which sounds ludicrous today—that the king's suffering was the result of excess abstemiousness. That doctor actually may have been right.

To investigate further:

Black, Jeremy. *George III: America's Last King.* New Haven, CT: Yale University Press, 2006. A simple, straightforward history of George's life and reign.

Deats-O'Reilly, Diana. *Porphyria, the Unknown Disease.* Grand Forks, ND: Porphyria Press, 1999. This book looks at the disease's causes, symptoms, and long-term effects.

Hibbert, Christopher. *George III: A Personal History.* New York: Basic Books, 1988. This well-written biography focuses on the king as a man, a husband, and a father.

Lloyd, Alan. *The King Who Lost America: A Portrait of the Life and Times of King George III.* New York: Doubleday, 2002. A good aid to understanding the complex relationship between king and country in an empire-building age.

Long, J. C. *George III: The Story of a Complex Man.* Boston: Little, Brown & Co., 1960. The subtitle describes the author's concern with little-understood aspects of the king's character and behavior.

MacAlpine, Ida, and Richard Hunter. *George III and the Mad-Business.* New York: Pantheon, 1969. The authors look at the king's illness and its impact upon politics and policy.

Plumb, J. H. *The First Four Georges.* London: Fontana Press, 1972. An efficient overview of Britain's eighteenth-century House of Hanover.

Rohl, John C. G., Martin Warren, and David Hunt. *Purple Secret: Genes, "Madness" and the Royal Houses of Europe.* London: Corgi, 1999. The author looks at hereditary porphyria as it affected not only George, but other members of his extended royal family.

13

Was George IV a Bigamist?

When is a marriage not a marriage? Wait, don't answer that. It sounds too much like the setup for a cynical punch line. How about this, then? A man pursues a woman. She comes to love him but self-respectfully refuses to become his conquest or his mistress. If he would have her, she demands that there must be a wedding. He agrees. In fact, he not only agrees, he insists. They recite vows before a clergyman, after which she devotes herself to him, forsaking all others. Yet she cannot be referred to as his wife. What, then, is she?

Some questions surrounding the nuptial status of George Augustus Frederick, the Prince of Wales, are more along the lines of a riddle than a mystery—although the workings of the human heart are ever mysterious. George married twice and never divorced. His first wife, Maria Fitzherbert, outlived him, so she was indubitably alive when he married for the second time, to his first cousin Caroline of Brunswick. Later he tried and failed to have his marriage to Caroline declared invalid. Maria, on the other hand, sought and received an official ruling that George was married to her and had never been married to Caroline. Many of their contemporaries in the late eighteenth and early nineteenth centuries found it confusing, but perhaps not as confusing as it all seems two hundred years later. Riddle us this: who was the prince's wife—Maria, Caroline, both, or neither?

The prince, later George IV of the United Kingdom, rebelled in his late teens against an overprotective, straitlaced upbringing as the son of George III, the only one of Britain's four Georges never to take a mistress (and probably one of very few kings anywhere, ever, to remain flawlessly faithful to his queen consort). To his sober-minded father's horror, George the younger, at about age seventeen, began to socialize with hard-drinking politicians of the reformist Whig Party. Even worse, by the king's standards, the heir apparent to the crown began throwing money around with abandon, while he also threw himself into the pursuit of aesthetic pleasures—especially pleasures of the flesh. Little Georgie quickly became accustomed to having what he wanted, and whom he wanted, when he wanted.

By age twenty-one, the prince had already enjoyed a series of mistresses—each, in turn, handsomely paid to leave him alone once he grew tired of her. He sired a number of illegitimate children. Then, early in 1784, he caught sight of the widow Fitzherbert's fashionably pale face and buxom figure at the Covent Garden Opera. Once again, George was smitten.

Mrs. Fitzherbert came from a prominent recusant family. That is, she was Catholic. That may sound irrelevant, but it's not. The English recusants were so called because of their refusal to attend services of the Church of England. By recusing themselves, they committed an offense not only against the church but also against the English state. These families, some quite wealthy and socially prominent, were subject to many discriminatory laws—even in the late eighteenth century, 250 years after Henry VIII broke the ties between the English church and Rome. Under the provisions of the Act of Settlement of 1701, not only Catholics but also those married to Catholics were barred from ascending to the throne. George I, the prince's great-great-grandfather, had not been the most direct royal descendent when he became king in 1714, but he had been the most direct *Protestant* royal descendent. This means that the royal family—at that time, the Hanover Dynasty—owed its fortunes to anti-Catholic feeling and anti-Catholic legislation.

Under the Act of Settlement, had George married Mrs. Fitzherbert, he would have taken himself out of the line of succession. By another law, the Royal Marriages Act of 1772, he couldn't legally marry her. That law prohibits any member of the royal family under the age of twenty-five from marrying without royal consent. The king, had he been consulted, would not have consented.

The prince pursued the socialite widow anyway. Perhaps without realizing it, she stoked his amorous fires by refusing his attentions. He wanted that which he could not have. Also, he was twenty-one and notoriously horny.

She, on the other hand, was twenty-seven and—though impeccably respectable—had been around. Maria Fitzherbert née Mary Anne Weld, née Mary Anne Smythe, was the granddaughter of a Hampshire baronet. At eighteen she had married Edward Weld, thirty-four, of a prominent Dorset recusant family. Not long afterward, Weld died, leaving her a widow before her twentieth birthday. Three years later, she married Thomas Fitzherbert, thirty-two, a Staffordshire nobleman and another recusant. (English Catholics of the time married virtually exclusively among themselves.) Fitzherbert, though a strapping, athletic sort, had tuberculosis. The couple traveled to Nice (now in France, but then in the kingdom of Savoy) in hopes that the Mediterranean climate would effect a cure. It did not. Fitzherbert died in Savoy in 1781, leaving his young widow a comfortable house in the fashionable Mayfair district of London and a generous private income.

Now calling herself by the continental moniker Maria, she established herself among the English capital's social set, where she came to the attention of her royal admirer. More level-headed than he and unwilling to throw away her good reputation, she was cordial and respectful to the amorous prince. She flirted with him, but only in the casual way that society beauties of the time habitually flirted with important men. It was something that one did. The self-possessed Mrs. Fitzherbert, confident of her beauty, did it well.

It wasn't that the widow didn't care for the prince. Like virtually every woman in London, Maria found him extremely handsome and charming. He possessed considerably more wit than did any other member of the royal family in living memory (which may not have been saying much). He was a talented and well-trained cellist and singer, and he was already making a reputation for himself as a tastemaker, especially for commissioning a stunning redesign for Carleton House, his London residence, from architect Henry Holland. Added to that, Maria became genuinely fond of young George—just not so fond that she would let him destroy her honor.

He sought her company, sent her expensive gifts, and wrote her dozens, if not hundreds, of flattering, entreating love letters. He commissioned artist Thomas Gainsborough to paint her portrait. Although she enjoyed the attention, Maria held fast. With a noblewoman friend, she planned a trip to France to let her royal suitor cool off.

On July 8, 1784, the evening before Maria was to leave, four men arrived at her house begging her to come to Carleton House. Among them was Prince George's physician and Lord Southampton, the head of the prince's household. They told her that the prince had stabbed himself, that he was in mortal danger, and that only her presence would save him. At first, she did not believe them. It seemed an obvious ploy. She knew that if she were to go by herself to visit the prince at his residence, it would amount to throwing away her respectability.

The men pleaded with her, describing the prince's self-inflicted wound as having just missed his heart and saying that he was so distraught for want of her love that they feared he would tear off his bandages and bleed to death. With difficulty, they convinced her that the prince really was injured, but she still insisted that she could not go to him. After more persuasion, she agreed to go, but only in the company of another respectable lady.

The group then collected the Duchess of Devonshire and proceeded by crowded carriage to Carleton House. There, Maria found the prince in bed, looking pale and with bloodstains on his shirt. He threw a tantrum, banging his head against the wall and claiming that his life was nothing without her. With reluctance, she agreed to let him put a ring on her finger, and she promised to marry him. He had been drinking, and she rather hoped that he wouldn't remember what had transpired.

Maria set out for Europe the next day, pausing only to write a letter of protest to Lord Southampton, expressing her feeling that she had not entered into an agreement of her own free will. She stayed on the continent until late the next year. The prince not only remembered the incident with the ring and the promise, he reminded her of his love, and of their contract, in letter after letter. Finally, she came to think that she must live in exile forever or agree to marry George. Although she knew she could never be queen and must have known that the prince could not publicly admit to their marriage, she went through with the ceremony—a private affair overseen by a Church of England priest—in December 1785.

The marriage was a secret, or was supposed to be. For purposes of state and for the preservation of his own future, the

Prince of Wales could not be married to Mrs. Fitzherbert. They did not live with each other but near each other—both in London and in the seaside resort of Brighton. They observed certain formalities of address and behavior in public. When confronted with the rumor of the marriage, George had his proxies issue vehement denials. In other words, he lied. It hurt Maria, but she stayed with him, at least until the mid-1790s.

Inevitably, given his character (or lack of), the prince drifted back to his old ways, taking up with other women. He continued to overspend, which led to massive debts, and to overdrink, which hardly improved his judgment. Realizing that Parliament would help him out of his financial scrape only if he took an official wife and produced an heir, George dropped Maria and agreed to wed his cousin Caroline, a German princess. Not only did he not love the princess, he found her presence objectionable. By many accounts, Caroline was sloppy and careless of hygiene to the point that she stank. Nonetheless, he married her, without bothering to do anything about his first marriage, as he could still pretend that it had never taken place. George and Caroline produced a daughter, Charlotte. George handed off the baby to royal nannies, and in 1799 he sent his wife away to a residence in Blackheath where he would not have to see or smell her—not that he'd seen much of her since the wedding night. There, the fun-loving Caroline entertained admirers and raised a little boy who some suspected was her son by a lover. In 1814 she moved to Italy.

Around 1800, the prince returned to Maria. She agreed to take him back, but only after she had sought, and received, a ruling from the Vatican in Rome. Pope Pius VII responded with assurances that Maria's marriage to George was both legitimate and insoluble. Even though the ceremony was conducted by an Anglican priest using the English prayer book, it was a Christian sacramental marriage in the eyes of the Roman Catholic Church. (It should be noted that the popes of this time were not inclined to make life any easier for Protestant English royalty.) The marriage to Caroline thus had never been valid.

In London, the George-Maria marriage remained publicly unacknowledged. It was a fact that everyone knew, but that everyone knew was officially not so. The marriage was still secret, and George was still George. While reconciling with Maria, he kept the notoriously libertine Frances Villiers, the Countess of Jersey, as his mistress. He also kept drinking and carousing. In 1811, the year that Parliament appointed George regent to take care of royal business in place of his by now irrevocably insane father (see the previous chapter), George and Maria parted for good.

Upon the death of his father in 1820, the no-longer-young prince became George IV, and his "official" wife, Caroline, returned to England from Italy, eager to take her place as queen consort. George IV refused to recognize her claim to the title. He tried to dissolve his marriage to her on grounds of her adultery until he realized that his own marital fidelity would not stand up under legal scrutiny. Then he tried to have Parliament annul the marriage, again on grounds of adultery, in a process that would not require a court of law. Caroline's answer to the charge of adultery was a classic. She admitted that she had once committed the offense, with the husband of Mrs. Fitzherbert.

She was popular with the English public. Caroline was, after all, the king's wife, and the masses enthusiastically hailed her as their new queen. There were riots in her support. Members of the House of Commons, being politicians, knew better than to wade into that dangerous territory. The parliamentary annulment failed.

Finally, the king simply barred her from his coronation in 1821. Caroline showed up at Westminster Cathedral, demanding to be admitted, but the guards wouldn't let her in. Was she the queen? By British law and tradition, yes. By George, no.

On the night of the coronation, Caroline fell ill with vomiting and abdominal pain. She died three weeks later at age fifty-three. Doctors said the cause was an intestinal obstruction. Caroline herself suspected poison, although the pattern of her affliction—a violent bout of illness that leads to death three weeks later—did not resemble most deaths by poison.

As for the king's never-dissolved marriage with Maria Fitzherbert, he apparently kept her foremost in his heart to the end of his life. The king died and was buried in 1830 with a miniature portrait of his "secret wife" upon a gold chain around his neck. In spirit, if not by law, he considered her to have been his true spouse. And the case can be made that although she could by law never be queen, she really *was* married to the king.

Author James Munson, in a biography of Maria Fitzherbert, points out that the 1785 marriage between George and Maria met all of the requirements for legal matrimony—not just in the eyes of the Vatican, but also under English law. That is, the priest—one Robert Burt—was legally ordained. There were the required witnesses. The man and the woman were of legal age and eligible to marry—he a bachelor, she a widow. They had entered into a contract with one another, with all the figurative t's crossed and i's dotted.

The Settlement Act said that the prince could not marry a Catholic and retain his claim to the crown. The act made it a crime for a priest to conduct such a ceremony and for English subjects to witness such a ceremony, but did any of that mean that the marriage itself, once solemnized, was invalid? The Royal Marriages Act said that the prince could not marry without his father's consent, yet he *had* married.

Undoubtedly, an English court would have found reason to formally declare the marriage of George and Maria invalid—for political, if not legal, reasons. Thus, the king's official marriage to Caroline of Brunswick would have been found valid, no matter how much George despised it (and, in fact, he had found that he couldn't get out of it). Yet the pope had formally ruled that the marriage of George and Maria was indeed valid and thus the marriage to Caroline was invalid. Either way, George was not a bigamist. He was certainly a bounder and a cad, but he was not, by either civil or cannon law, a bigamist.

The two real unsolved mysteries surrounding George and his wife are the kind that no one is ever likely to solve. In fact, there seems to be no way to investigate them. One is whether the king had anything to do with Queen Caroline's conveniently timed death. Judging by the course of her illness, this seems highly unlikely but not impossible. Unless and until a bit of evidence can be found, and none yet has, George must be presumed innocent of that one.

The other mystery is less consequential but perhaps more interesting. Did Prince George, on that ridiculously melodramatic evening in 1784, really attempt to kill himself? In later years, Mrs. Fitzherbert assured others that his blood and anguish had been real and that she had seen the scar. Doubters point out that the prince knew how to use a medical lancet to bleed himself— a practice considered at the time to be a good therapy for fever. As for the lasting mark upon his breast, perhaps the prince was aware of the cosmetic practice, especially among certain vain Prussian military officers, of giving oneself a dramatic "fencing" scar. The same technique might serve, especially to the untrained eye of a socialite widow, as evidence of a suicide attempt.

To investigate further:

Baker, Kenneth. *George IV: A Life in Caricature*. London: Thames & Hudson, 2005. The author, a former British cabinet member, explores and celebrates the monarch's life and times in a book that is beautifully illustrated with vintage political cartoons.

Haeger, Diane. *The Secret Wife of George IV*. New York: St. Martin's Griffin, 2000. A historical novel imagines the private life of Mrs. Fitzherbert.

Irvine, Valerie. *The King's Wife: George IV and Mrs. Fitzherbert*. London: Hambledon & London, 2005. A readable account of the king's marriage makes the point that his bond with Mrs. Fitzherbert may have been the most genuine human relationship he ever experienced.

Munson, James. *Maria Fitzherbert: The Secret Wife of George IV*. New York: Carroll & Graf, 2001. Mostly a biography of Mrs. Fitzherbert, this history illuminates the workings of late-eighteenth-century London society and politics.

Parissien, Steven. *George IV: Inspiration of the Regency*. New York: St. Martin's Press, 2002. The author does not ignore his subject's copious faults but does not let them obscure the king's considerable talents.

Plowright, John. *Regency England: The Age of Lord Liverpool*. New York: Routledge, 1996. A look at the period from another perspective, that of an influential politician.

Priestley, J. B. *The Prince of Pleasure and His Regency, 1811–20*. New York: Harper & Row, 1969. The prince regent's propensity for self-indulgence comes to the fore.

Smith, E. A. *George IV*. New Haven, CT: Yale University Press, 1999. A no-nonsense, even-handed biography.

14

What Happened to the Lost Dauphin of France?

Pity little Louis-Charles, a victim of revolution and circumstance. He had the ill fortune to be born into royalty at one of the most inopportune moments in history. The second son of Louis XVI was four years old when the French Revolution broke out and was only age seven when the revolutionary government overthrew the monarchy.

Louis-Charles, the second son and the third child of King Louis and Queen Marie Antoinette, became dauphin, the title borne by the heir to the throne, when his older brother, Louis-Joseph, died of tuberculosis in June 1789. About a month later, on July 14, a Parisian mob stormed the Bastille, a state prison that had become, for France's increasingly dissatisfied masses, a symbol of Bourbon tyranny. (The Bourbons, little Louis-Charles's family, were the ruling dynasty of France.) Three years later, the revolutionary government toppled the king and locked the royal family into cells in the Temple, which, like the Bastille, was an ancient Parisian fortress used as a prison.

In December 1792, the National Convention—then the legislative body of the revolutionary government—convicted Louis XVI of treason for conspiring with enemy states Austria and Prussia and with exiled French nobles to restore the Bourbon monarchy. The delegates voted that the deposed king, whom they referred to as "Citizen Capet," must die. (Capet had been the byname of the dynasty's tenth-century founder, Hugh Capet.) In early 1793, the revolutionaries carted Capet to the guillotine and sliced off his head. Eight-year-old Louis-Charles instantly became—at least, in the minds of French monarchists—Louis XVII. This was during the Reign of Terror, when heads were being chopped off left and right, but mostly right. Noble birth alone could get a person beheaded. It wasn't a great time to be the "rightful" king of France. Fittingly, the twenty-first-century *Chicago Reader* column "The Straight Dope" (which often covers historical subjects) has dubbed the little prince "Unlucky Chucky."

The boy couldn't win. He represented both a danger to the revolution and a potentially valuable property to the revolutionaries. They had something that royalist counterrevolutionaries wanted. There was also the prospect, irresistible to egalitarian leftists, of taking this pampered palace pup and making an example of him. That summer, jailers pried the child from the arms of his mother, Marie Antoinette. She is said to have clung to him ferociously, only letting go when her captors threatened to kill both Louis-Charles and his teenage sister, Marie Thérèse-Charlotte, if the mother did not surrender the boy. He was put under the charge of a cobbler who was housed in the Temple. The boy's position was akin to that of an apprentice. According to antirevolutionary monarchists, he was ill-treated and mocked. Other accounts say that the cobbler's wife looked after the boy and saw that he was clean and fed. The truth may lie somewhere in between. In either account, his captors coerced the boy into signing an accusation of treason directed against his mother.

That fall, the government brought Marie Antoinette before a revolutionary tribunal, convicted her of treason, and sentenced her to the same fate as her late husband, beheading by guillotine. A few months later, the cobbler and his wife left the Temple, and the prince was put back into a prison cell. Some say he was already seriously ill by this time, too ill to work and too ill to be used as a bargaining chip in negotiations with royalist enemies. Other say he was in good health and only fell ill, suddenly, later. Either way, he reportedly died of scrofula (tuberculosis of the lymph glands) on June 8, 1795. The body was thrown into a mass grave. Again, reportedly.

That would have been the end of the tale of the young dauphin—a sad example of child abuse in the name of revolutionary zeal. It would have been, except that there were many French people, and many abroad as well, who either could not or would not believe it. Although prison inspectors supposedly looked in on the ten-year-old dauphin during his last months, it's not certain how he fared. Sensationalist, antirevolutionary accounts depicted him during this time as barricaded in his cell, completely isolated, shivering on the cold stone floor as he lay ill and filthy, infested by skin mites that raised red rashes all over his body. Whatever his condition, it is likely that the child felt miserable and lonely.

When a well-known figure, whether famous or notorious, disappears from public view, people will always speculate. Think of American aviator Amelia Earhart in the twentieth century. Deprived of a satisfactory conclusion and lacking proof of what really happened, the public substitutes a story.

Rumors arose in the 1790s that the boy had escaped. A royalist sympathizer—in some versions, a royalist noble; in others, the cobbler's wife—was supposed to have smuggled him out of the prison and out of France, maybe to Austria. He was still alive, said the hopeful. The emaciated little corpse that was later carted from the cell had not been that of Louis-Charles, they said; it was another boy. Sick and on the edge of death, the second boy had been switched with the dauphin to facilitate the dauphin's escape. In more elaborate tellings, including the complicated version told by one Karl Wilhelm Naundorff, the most credible of many men who later claimed to be the escaped prince, there were stages of substitution. At first, his rescuers smuggled the boy to another part of the Temple, substituting a wooden figure in his cell. Then, because they knew the wooden prince would not fool the guards for long, they found a deaf-mute boy to live in the cell. Finally, they substituted the corpse of yet another boy for purposes of the death certificate.

Such a story, about a young prince or princess surviving against impossible odds, has powerful appeal. (See chapters 5 and 18.) Royalists wanted to believe that the legitimate heir to the crown was out there somewhere, awaiting his chance to return in triumph. Sentimentalists wanted to believe that the little boy had somehow survived the abuse and found freedom and happiness. Even believers in republicanism wanted to avoid thinking of the revolution as a cruel persecutor of children. "People preferred a happy ending," said French historian Philippe Delorme, talking to reporters in 2004 about a scientific attempt to solve the two-hundred-year-old mystery.

If the dauphin had been rescued, where was he? None of his royal relatives admitted having taken him in. France had been ruled by the Bourbon Dynasty since 1589, and at the end of the eighteenth century, Bourbon rulers continued to reign in Spain (and not just mainly in the plain), as well as in Parma, Naples, and Sicily. On his mother's side, the young dauphin was related to the Hapsburgs, rulers of much of the rest of Europe. It seems impossible that the child, had he survived, would not have taken refuge in a palace in some European capital, virtually anywhere but France.

Yet Europe was at war almost continually from 1792 to 1815. France's revolutionary wars blended into the Napoleonic Wars. By 1795, France was pushing its neighbors back on every front and gaining hegemony over most of the continent. A safe place for a French prince might not have been easy to find. Whoever had rescued the dauphin may have decided that there was good reason to keep his survival a secret. What if the royal refugee had been harbored not in a palace but in a cottage or a stout middle-class house in Germany, or even somewhere as unlikely as a Caribbean island or a Mohawk village in Canada?

There was no shortage of explanations for where the boy had been stashed. This was because dozens of young men claiming to be the lost dauphin emerged in the early decades of the nineteenth century. Most estimates say there were at least thirty claimants and some say as many as a hundred. The public saw most of these candidates for what they were: clumsy frauds seeking wealth, fame, power—or, in most cases, all three.

John James Audubon was an exception. If the American artist and ornithologist ever claimed to be Louis-Charles, he seems to have done it largely because he found the idea amusing. The very notion that naturalist Audubon could be the dauphin arose because (1) he was about the right age, (2) he grew up in France, and (3) his origins were vaguely mysterious.

Audubon was born not in France but in the French colony of Saint-Domingue, which is now Haiti. His mother, Jeanne Rabin, was not married to his father, a sea trader and plantation owner. A resident of Saint-Domingue, Jeanne may have been the elder Audubon's slave. The father returned to Europe and the Lorraine region of France sometime around 1790. Later he sent for the boy and another child, a girl whom he had fathered by a different island woman. In Nancy, a town in Lorraine, Audubon and his wife, Anne, formally adopted the children in 1794. They had the boy christened Jean-Jacques Fougère Audubon. In 1803, his father sent young Jean-Jacques to the United States to keep him from being drafted into Napoleon's massive French army, which was conscripting every man and boy who proved able to carry a weapon. In America, the young man anglicized his name to John James. Yet the French background, the 1794 adoption, and his virtually anonymous birth invited speculation about who the gifted artist and scientist might *really* be.

There is evidence of his sense of humor, and of his attitude toward the rumor that he was the dauphin, in a droll letter that the mature naturalist wrote to his wife from Paris while visiting there in 1828. He mused about strolling through the French capital, behaving like an ordinary person, bowing to others in the place where all should bow to him. It's extremely unlikely that he intended such comments to be taken seriously.

Another American, Eleazar Williams, gained fame as the "lost dauphin" rather late in life. In 1853 *Putnam's* magazine published an article titled "Have We a Bourbon among Us?" by John H. Hanson. The piece somehow struck a nerve among the American reading public. *Putnam's* circulation soared. The next year, Hanson followed with a full-length book titled *The Lost Prince*. Hanson told the story of a child spirited away from France in the mid-1790s and taken by ship to Canada, where he was placed in the care of a Mohawk woman, Mary Ann Williams, who raised him among her people. Later this unheralded prince had moved to New England, then to New York, and then the Michigan territory. The book was a best seller. Americans wanted to believe that the king of France had lived as an American citizen, an everyman.

Williams, however, was no everyman. The colorful character was indeed Mohawk by heritage and upbringing, although he was also descended, on his mother's side, from a prominent Boston family. Differing accounts have him attending either Dartmouth College in Hanover, New Hampshire, or else a charity academy for Indian youths that was associated with the college. The latter is more likely true, and he probably did not stay long. He served in the War of 1812, although the stories he later told of his exploits as a scout and a spy sound suspiciously exaggerated.

Williams had a lifelong habit of stretching the truth, especially when it came to his own identity and origins. As early as 1810, he occasionally seems to have claimed to be descended from French nobility. It's somewhat ironic that Williams would invent a fictional past, considering that the man's real origins were remarkably interesting. He was the great-grandson of Eunice Williams, a cousin of the great Boston clergyman and writer Cotton Mather. As a child, Eunice had been taken hostage by the Mohawk tribe in 1704 and had remained with the tribe. Eunice had taken a Mohawk husband who adopted her family name. One of their children, Sarah Williams, was Eleazar's grandmother.

Eleazar Williams's early career was also notable, if not entirely admirable. He became an Episcopal missionary to the Oneida and other tribes in New York State and then organized an effort to move Eastern tribes westward into what was then Michigan Territory. The drive was financed by a land company eager to take over the Native Americans' New York farms. Williams probably profited financially from the deal, although his principal motivation appears to have been a dream to establish, and personally rule, an Indian empire in the American Midwest, centered in what would later be northern Wisconsin. Only after that plan fell through did a bankrupt Williams begin his campaign to be accepted as the lost dauphin.

Author Hanson, a fellow clergyman, had first met Williams on a train in 1851. He was impressed by Williams's supposed facial resemblance to the French royal family and by an elaborate story that Williams, by then in his sixties, had been spinning for at least a decade previously. Had he known Williams longer, Hanson might have been a bit more skeptical.

Even well after Williams's death in 1858, some believers clung to the idea that he had been the dauphin or at least fixated on the possibility that it might have been true. An 1868 article in *Putnam's* bore the title "Louis XVII and Eleazar Williams: Were They Really the Same Person?" Novelist Mark Twain, however, sent up the very idea of duplicitous American adventurers claiming European titles when he created the hilarious characters of the Duke and the Dauphin in his 1884 novel *The Adventures of Huckleberry Finn*. The elderly grifter Dauphin, whom Huck refers to as "the king," appears to be a fictionalized version of Williams.

Despite Twain and other skeptics, the Mohawk Bourbon achieved at least a certain level of official acceptance. A state historical marker at Lost Dauphin State Park near De Pere, Wisconsin, where Williams had labored to found his Indian empire, asks earnestly, "Was he the lost Dauphin?"

Naundorff's marker, his gravestone in the Netherlands, is far less tentative. It names the occupant as "Louis XVII, roi de France et de Navarre (Charles Louis, duc de Normandie)," translated as "Louis XVII, king of France and Navarre (Charles Louis, duke of Normandy)," and his Dutch death certificate lists him as "Charles Louis de Bourbon, duc de Normandie."

Nothing is known about Naundorff's birth or upbringing. He arrived in 1810 in Berlin, where he applied for and was granted Prussian citizenship. He worked as a watchmaker, and later, in the nearby town of Brandenburg, he was convicted of counterfeiting coins and served a three-year jail sentence. By the late 1820s, Naundorff had begun to introduce himself as the Duke of Burgundy. He wrote and published two books that he said were memoirs of his childhood, imprisonment, and escape. His story, like Williams's, included being smuggled to America—although in Naundorff's version, the kidnappers had brought him back to Europe.

Unlike Williams—who claimed amnesia about his early life—Naundorff knew a great deal about the royal family, its residences, and its daily life. He traveled from Germany to France, where his knowledge was enough to convince at least a few former members of Louis XVI's court—most notably, the woman who had been the young dauphin's nurse—that he was the real thing. She said that she recognized a mole and specific scars, including one on his upper lip where a pet rabbit had bitten the toddler Louis-Charles.

He did not, however, convince Princess Marie-Thérèse-Charlotte, the elder sister of the dauphin and the only survivor among those royals who had been imprisoned in the Temple. After seeing a picture of Naundorff, she refused to meet with him. In 1836 he tried to sue her but was unsuccessful.

In retrospect, Naundorff looks like another crackpot, but at the time his threat to the surviving Bourbons, and to France, stirred strong feelings. Twice in Paris, he narrowly escaped attempts on his life. And when he died of a sudden illness in 1845, supporters said that he had been poisoned.

Naundorff's claim did not die with him. Over the following decades, his sons and grandsons filed numerous petitions for recognition from the French government. As late as 1954, a French court denied such a claim, filed by a descendent who called himself René Charles de Bourbon.

In late 1999, a French team of molecular geneticists attempted to settle the issue for good by analyzing the DNA of a preserved heart attributed to Louis-Charles—or at least to the boy who was buried under that name. The heart had a complicated story of its own. Supposedly, Dr. Philippe-Jean Pelletan, the physician who was called to conduct an autopsy on the deceased Louis-Charles, had cut out the boy's heart. It sounds gruesome, but there was a tradition in many European monarchies, a tradition that predated Christianity, of removing a king's heart and entombing it separately from the rest of the body.

Pelletan said that he took the heart away, hidden in his handkerchief, and preserved it in a jar of alcohol in his study. There, one of his anatomy students apparently found the royal relic too tempting to resist and stole it. Upon his deathbed, the student repented and asked that the heart be returned to Pelletan. Instead, the man's widow sent the heart to the archbishop of Paris. As the story goes, the urn containing the heart was smashed during the July Revolution of 1830 (when Charles X, last of the Bourbons, was overthrown in favor of his distant cousin Louis-Philippe). The heart was rescued from the shards of glass. It also spent some time in the possession of the Spanish branch of the Bourbon family before being returned to a royal crypt in Paris in 1975.

The scientists had no way of confirming whether the small heart they took from the crypt in 1999 was the same one taken from the boy, but they were able to establish that its DNA matched that found in hair samples taken from members of the Bourbon family, including some preserved hair attributed to Marie-Antoinette, taken from her during her childhood in Austria. In other words, there was no doubt that this was the heart of a member of the French royal family.

The mystery appeared to have been solved, although room for doubt remained. What if the heart had been taken not from the boy who died in the cell but from his older brother, Louis-Joseph, who died before him in 1789? It also would match. Yet French historian Delorme, who helped to arrange the scientific tests, told reporters that it was improbable that the heart belonged to the older prince, as Louis-Joseph's heart was unlikely to have been preserved in alcohol, as this one was.

Similar tests conducted on a bit of bone and hair that had been taken from Naundorff's grave in the 1950s showed no such genetic link to either Marie Antoinette or to hair samples from two of her sisters. The scientists used mitochondrial DNA, which, unlike the DNA in a cell's nucleus, passes its nucleotide sequences unchanged from a mother to her children, generation after generation.

The test results have not deterred Naundorff's family. His descendents maintain a Web site devoted to their cause of proving royal lineage. And in 2006, a Dutch-born, retired Canadian realtor who calls himself Prince Charles de Bourbon self-published a book titled *I Exist*, in which he tells his life story and details his family claim to royal descent. De Bourbon dismisses the DNA tests. Along with other critics of the tests, he charges that the heart attributed to the imprisoned boy may have been taken, instead, from the chest of one of the Spanish Bourbons, and that its handling over two hundred years certainly makes it likely to have been contaminated. The bits of matter taken from Naundorff's grave also had not been properly preserved, he charges, and had been badly contaminated before the testing. He calls for the tomb to be opened again so that new tests can be carried out on uncontaminated tissue.

To investigate further:

Cadbury, Deborah. *The Lost King of France: How DNA Solved the Mystery of the Murdered Son of Louis XVI and Marie Antoinette*. New York: St. Martin's Griffin, 2003. The long subtitle adequately describes this scientific-historical sleuth tale.

Carlyle, Thomas, and John D. Rosenberg. *The French Revolution: A History*. New York: Modern Library, 2004. A solid, chronological narrative of the events that tore a society to its foundations.

De Bourbon, Prince Charles. *I Exist*. Victoria, British Columbia: Trafford Publishing, 2006. A descendant of Karl Wilhelm Naundorff stakes his claim to royal ancestry in this self-published book.

Fraser, Antonia. *Marie Antoinette: The Journey*. New York: Nan A. Talese/ Doubleday, 2001. A sympathetic and well-written biography of the queen.

Hanson, John H. *The Lost Prince: Facts Tending to Prove the Identity of Louis the Seventeenth, of France, and the Rev. Eleazar Williams, Missionary among the Indians of North America*. Ann Arbor: University of Michigan, 2005. A reprint of a vintage best seller arguing in favor of Williams's claim to dauphin identity.

Jones, Colin. *The Great Nation: France from Louis XV to Napoleon*. New York: Columbia University Press, 2003. This sweeping narrative brings an entire century of history into brilliant focus.

Meyer, Anna. *The DNA Detectives: How the Double Helix Is Solving Puzzles of the Past*. New York: Thunder's Mouth Press, 2006. The dauphin DNA case is included among other historical-scientific inquiries.

Rhodes, Richard. *John James Audubon: The Making of an American*. New York: Vintage, 2006. A biography of the pioneering artist-naturalist.

15

Was Napoleon Poisoned?

In 1821, Napoleon Bonaparte, the most famous person of his era, and among the most famous in history, died in exile on St. Helena, a remote island in the Atlantic Ocean. He was fifty-one. Inevitably, questions arose.

Francesco Antommarchi, the Corsican physician who conducted the autopsy, listed stomach cancer as the cause of death. Cancer can fell anyone at any stage of life, but some partisans of the man who crowned himself Napoleon I—whose titles had included emperor of the French, king of Italy, mediator of the Swiss Confederation, and protector of the Confederation of the Rhine—thought of him as virtually superhuman. They found it difficult to believe that a mere disease, much less a sickness of the tummy, could have stilled the dynamo. They suspected that someone among his many enemies had gotten away with murder.

How would a killer quietly do away with the deposed, although still high-profile, monarch to make it seem as if he died of a natural cause? The obvious means would be poison. In the early nineteenth century, that poison would most likely have been white arsenic. Also called arsenious oxide, the compound is tasteless. Investigators of the era were not able to detect it in a body. It was widely available and widely used for a variety of purposes, including discreet murder.

No one has established definitively that foul play killed Napoleon, although there are latter-day enthusiasts who claim to have made the case. The easy part is establishing motive. Although Napoleon's fabled military and political career won him fanatical supporters, he also made bitter enemies, many of whom may have craved revenge. Born on the Italian island of Corsica, Napoleon had been educated in France, where he became a military officer. During the French Revolution, most officers remained royalists, but Napoleon agreed to fight for the Republic, which was under attack by surrounding nations. Adept against foreign enemies, and also able to disperse Paris mobs, he helped to quell disorder to pave the way for the reformist Directory government in 1795. After several military adventures, he joined the 1799 plot to bring down the by then unpopular Directory. The next government was the Consulate, supposedly headed by a triumvirate. Napoleon was first among the three consuls, then was consul for life and sole ruler. In 1804 he won a popular vote that made him emperor.

Napoleon's troops not only defended their volatile nation, but also turned the tables on its enemies. Napoleon took control of vast swaths of Europe. The continent repeatedly exploded in turmoil during his reign—an era remembered as the Napoleonic Wars. During twenty-three years of conflict, culminating with the Battle of Waterloo in 1815, Britain and France were the bitterest and most constant of enemies.

After his final defeat at Waterloo, Napoleon surrendered himself to the British, asking for asylum. He proposed living out his life as an English country gentleman. Fat chance (or words to that effect), replied the government in London. Instead, the Brits shipped him to St. Helena, a remote island colony. It lies literally in the middle of the Atlantic Ocean—equidistant between Africa and South America. Napoleon's keepers wanted to be sure that he stayed put. During a previous exile, he'd been sent to another, more pleasant, and less remote island in the Mediterranean. From that island, Elba, he easily sailed back to France, raised an army, and staged a comeback that lasted more than three months.

So Britain's leaders were determined to keep Napoleon under their collective thumb, secure on the damp and foggy bump in the mid-Atlantic. He was there very much against his will and to the detriment, the emperor thought, of his health. "I have been murdered by the British oligarchy," he wrote in his will.

His hosts accommodated Napoleon and his attendants— servants, secretaries, courtiers, and so on—in a house called Longwood, built for the island's lieutenant governor. It was grand, if not palatial, but the emperor was far from comfortable there. He was bored and frustrated. He chafed under the watchful eye of the island's officious governor, Sir Hudson Lowe, who worried that Napoleon would try to escape.

Perhaps when Napoleon wrote, "I have been murdered," he meant that the isolation and the monotony of his life on St. Helena had weighed upon his spirits, drained him of energy, and robbed him of his will to live. Yet the emperor had always been deeply distrustful of others' motives, even to the point of paranoia. Was he leveling a literal accusation of murder at Lowe and his officers? Was it a credible accusation? If so, little besides rumors and vague recriminations came of it in the years and decades directly following the captive's death.

A serious challenge to Antommarchi's finding of stomach cancer rose only in the mid-twentieth century, when Swedish dentist Sten Forshufvud began a campaign to establish that the emperor had indeed been murdered. Forshufvud, a Napoleon fanatic, in the 1950s read a memoir written by Louis March- and, who had been Napoleon's valet on St. Helena. The Swede thought that the symptoms described by the valet—including weakness, abdominal pain, and vomiting—sounded suspiciously like those of chronic arsenic poisoning. They could also be the symptoms of many other ailments, but Forshuvfud was sure he was on to something. He reasoned that for chronic poisoning to have occurred, the substance would have had to be adminis- tered in gradual doses over time—probably over the course of Napoleon's exile—to mimic long-term illness.

Forshufvud saw another clue in the reported state of Napoleon's body when it was disinterred from a St. Helena grave in 1820. (The French government had arranged to bring the re- mains to Paris.) Witnesses reported that the corpse appeared remarkably well preserved, as if it had been in the ground only a few days instead of nineteen years. This fed Forshufvud's sus- picion about the cause of death, because arsenic has sometimes been used as a preservative in tanning hides and in taxidermy. Thus, an unusually high level of arsenic in a body's tissues might be expected to slow a corpse's decomposition.

Seeking to prove that the emperor was poisoned, Foshufvud obtained a sample of hair that reputedly was Napoleon's. He arranged for forensic scientists at Glasgow University in Scot- land to test the hair, and the results were a finding of unusually high concentrations of arsenic. The Swede wrote a book titled *Who Killed Napoleon?* in which he stated his case. Historians dismissed it, but Forshufvud continued to argue for his theory over subsequent decades.

Ben Weider, a multifaceted Canadian business executive whose pursuits range from bodybuilding to French history, also believed in the poisoning theory. In the 1970s he joined Forshufvud's campaign to convince others, especially academic historians, that the emperor had been killed. Tests of more hairs that supposedly were Napoleon's (he had given them out as keepsakes) showed evidence of long-term arsenic intake. Weider wrote about the topic in his own books and with Forshufvud coauthored 1995's *Assassination at St. Helena Revisited.*

Traditionalists were not swayed, especially not in France, where the official cause of death remained stomach cancer. But by the end of the twentieth century, some mainstream Napoleon scholars had adopted the poison theory. For example, in his 1997 biography, historian Alan Schom wrote, "The autopsy results notwithstanding, there is no doubt that Napoleon was murdered." If this is true, who did it?

Although Napoleon may have pointed a finger at Sir Hudson, there seems no good reason to suspect St. Helena's governor or his superiors in London. The British had little to gain by killing their prominent prisoner. For the sake of international relations, they would have preferred to keep him alive, healthy, and irrelevant—safely tucked away—rather than promote him to martyrdom. Of course, individual British subjects—soldiers who had lost comrades and parents who had lost sons in the recent wars—had reason to hate Napoleon. One of them may have wanted to kill him, but how many had the opportunity?

Many latter-day inspectors see a better suspect in Charles Tristan, the Marquis de Montholon, who was a member of Napoleon's household throughout his stay on St. Helena. Tristan was often the emperor's closest companion, joining him at meals and over drinks. He had many chances to administer poison.

Why would Tristan commit such a crime? Schom writes that the motive was financial, that Tristan was an avaricious and scheming hanger-on who had only cozied up to Napoleon in hopes of gaining a large inheritance. Schon thinks that the noble simply wanted to speed along what he expected to be a financial windfall. Biographer Frank McLynn agrees that Tristan was greedy but proposes that he acted as a paid undercover agent and assassin, employed by French monarchists. This line of reasoning supposes that supporters of the Bourbon Dynasty resorted to hired murder to eliminate Napoleon as a claimant to the throne.

Author Frank Giles has discussed another motive, the speculation that Tristan was a jealous husband, murderously angry over an affair between his wife and the emperor (although some accounts suggest that Tristan willingly shared his wife's affections). Another domestic theory has it that Tristan missed his wife terribly. Having tired of St. Helena, she had returned to Paris. In this scenario, Napoleon's death would have been a way for the killer to end his obligation so that he could go home and reunite with her.

Most supporters of the poisoning theory believe that arsenic weakened but did not finish Napoleon. Many believe that his doctors delivered the final blow by administering medications in inappropriate doses and combinations. These included tartar emetic, the purgative calomel, and a bitter almond drink, orgeat, that was intended to quench the patient's raging thirst. McLynn and Weider have written that the calomel and the orgeat could have reacted with each another, forming deadly mercury cyanide in the patient's stomach. Too much tartar emetic, with the resultant vomiting, could have caused a severe potassium deficiency.

Would the long-term arsenic exposure have to be malicious? Could it have been an accident? White arsenic was used widely in the early nineteenth century, as an ingredient in face powder, hair preparations, and medications. Vintners—including amateur wine-maker Napoleon—used the powdery chemical to dry their casks. Printers, textile manufacturers, and decorators used it in inks, dyes, and paints.

In 1982, David E. H. Jones theorized in a *Nature* magazine article that Napoleon might have been poisoned by the wallpaper at Longwood. Jones had obtained a sample of wallpaper attributed to the house during the years when the emperor lived there. Chemical analysis showed that the green pigment in the paper contained arsenic. In a damp climate like the island's, the wallpaper could have become moldy. A mold, Jones wrote, would break down the arsenic in the dye, transforming it into toxic dimethyl arsine and trimethyl arsine, which would be released in the air. If Napoleon spent a great deal of time indoors, as history reports he did in his last years, he might have been exposed to enough of this poison for it to have destroyed his health.

Murder theorists reject that line of reasoning. If the poison-by-wallpaper hypothesis were true, they argue, then other members of the household would have breathed in just as much of the gas. There isn't sufficient evidence of such exposure. And accidental exposure, they say, wouldn't have resulted in levels of arsenic in the hair that, according to Weider, reached a high of 51.2 parts per million (compared to a normal for the time of .08 parts per million).

Napoleon enthusiast Bob Elmer, in an article on the Napoleon Series Web site, offers another way for the emperor to have taken in, gradually, a large and potentially lethal amount of poison. Elmer suggests that Napoleon used arsenic as a recreational drug. Some thrill-seeking Europeans of the time deliberately consumed small doses of the poison. They claimed that it gave them a feeling of well-being and sexual stamina. Elmer thinks it possible that Napoleon, bored by his restricted life in exile, began to take arsenic for kicks. As he developed a tolerance, he would have increased his dosage to get the desired effect, and the poison would have eventually taken its toll.

Whatever ruined Napoleon's health, it did not reduce him to skin and bones. Antommarchi's autopsy report noted a generous, uniform layer of fat under the skin. Poison theorists have cited this as further evidence against stomach cancer as the cause of death. That affliction, they argue, would have left the emperor emaciated.

Yet according to a 2005 announcement by a team of Swiss researchers, Napoleon's weight at the time of his death, given what it was before he fell ill, was precisely in keeping with a diagnosis of stomach cancer.

The researchers, based at medical institutes in Basel and Zurich, determined this by comparing the waistbands of twelve pairs of trousers worn by the emperor over the last twenty years of his life. Napoleon's pants, tailor-made, reflect his changing waistline. Using the emperor's girth and height (5 feet, 6½ inches), along with other calculations, they estimated him to weigh 148 pounds in 1800. He gained 50 pounds over the next two decades. Near the end, he dropped from 198 to 174 pounds, a sudden loss of 24 pounds. The doctors compared their data to weight changes among a group of 270 male patients. They also compared Antommarchi's 1821 measurement of the body's fat layer with the stomach fat found in modern patients who were killed by stomach cancer. They concluded that Napoleon's final weight loss was just what it would have been if he had indeed died of stomach cancer.

Later that same year, the beleaguered Dr. Antommarchi received another posthumous boost in the form of a manuscript found in a cottage in southern Scotland. It appeared to have been written by a British military doctor who signed it with the initials "J.C. Mc," and dated it "6th July 1821." Steve Lee, a military specialist for the British auction house of Thomson, Roddick, and Metcalf, told news reporters that the papers, two sheets of foolscap covered with a small, precise script, contain an eyewitness account of Napoleon's autopsy that spring. The doctor reported that he inspected the body carefully, especially the internal organs, and that the stomach was "the entire seat of the disease, which was a cancer or a schirrous [hard, fibrous] state of that viscus [organ]." He also said that the disease, having proceeded to such an advanced stage, must have been very painful.

Lee told reporters in 2005 that Dr. Mc's account should put an end to alternate theories about Napoleon's death. Yes, of course, just as the Battle of Waterloo put an end to war.

To investigate further:

Cronin, Vincent. *Napoleon Bonaparte: An Intimate Biography*. New York: William Morrow, 2001. The author's examination of the private Napoleon helps to illuminate his public persona.

Forshufvud, Sten. *Who Killed Napoleon?* London: Hutchinson & Co., 1961. This enthusiast was a lone voice when he began a campaign to prove that the emperor was poisoned.

Jones, R. Ben. *Napoleon: Man and Myth*. New York: Holmes & Meier, 1977. A readable biography, but it's best for the reader who is already somewhat familiar with the topic.

Martineau, Gilbert. *Napoleon's St. Helena*. New York: Rand McNally, 1966. The author focuses on the emperor's exile.

Schom, Alan. *Napoleon Bonaparte*. New York: HarperCollins, 1997. This well-written and psychologically astute biography depicts the emperor as a man of many contradictions.

Weider, Ben, and Sten Forshufvud. *Assassination at St. Helena Revisited*. New York: John Wiley & Sons, 1995. Advocates of the poisoning theory work together to argue their case.

Weider, Ben. *The Murder of Napoleon*. New York: Congdon & Lattes, 1982. Businessman-bodybuilder Weider's entry into the field.

16

Was Queen Victoria Sleeping with Her Servant?

I t's no secret that Queen Victoria felt a deep affection for her
Scottish servant, John Brown. When Brown died in 1883, she
mourned him with a sorrow akin to that she had expressed
for her worshipped husband, Prince Albert, after his death two
decades earlier. "The shock—the blow, the blank, the constant
missing at every turn of the one strong, powerful reliable arm
and head almost stunned me and I am truly overwhelmed," she
wrote. She made a shrine of Brown's room, placing a flower on
his bed every day for the rest of her life. She commissioned a
memorial statue of the man and tried to commission a biography
of him. When the writer she had chosen tactfully declined, she
thought of writing the book herself, until cooler heads wisely
dissuaded her. Yet even another two decades after that, at her
death in 1901, she left instructions that a picture of Brown and
a ring that he gave her be placed in her coffin, in her left hand.
Mementoes of Albert were in her right hand.

Clearly, this attachment between queen and commoner had been something extraordinary, at the very least an emotionally intimate friendship. Many of the queen's contemporaries thought it was also more than that, perhaps a romantic or even an intimately sexual partnership. Some even said, and a few wrote, that the queen and Brown, her personal attendant, had been secretly married.

When a woman shows a particular fondness for a man and spends a great deal of time alone with him, in private, rumors are inevitable. When that woman is the queen of the United Kingdom and Ireland and the empress of India, the interest intensifies. When the man is a low-born, rough-hewn, plain-spoken, uneducated Scot, and when the queen clearly favors him over other servants, not to mention over government ministers, diplomats, and even her own children, her fancy will undoubtedly breed jealousy, resentment, and perhaps a bit of moral outrage. The rumors are sure to intensify. Yet just because it's rumored doesn't mean that something is not true.

John Brown was born on a farm near Crathie, Aberdeenshire, in December 1826, making him a bit more than seven years younger than Queen Victoria. As a young man, he took a job at nearby Balmoral Castle as a gillie (also spelled ghillie), an outdoor servant who assists in activities such as riding and shooting. Victoria and Prince Albert first stayed at Balmoral in 1848 and were so taken with the surrounding peaceful yet rugged countryside that they purchased the castle and the estate in 1853. Brown stayed on, becoming Albert's personal gillie. The prince found that he could rely on this tall, sturdily built Highlander in any situation. He trusted Brown enough to assign him to be the queen's protector when she took outings, such as a ride in her pony cart, an activity she enjoyed.

In autumn of 1861, Albert contracted typhoid fever and died. During his twenty-one years of marriage, this German-born prince had become virtually indispensable to the queen.

He served as her private secretary and as her "permanent adviser," as he put it. He shaped her politics, her social philosophy, and even her personal habits and tastes. Albert's influence transformed her from the indolent, city-dwelling partygoer that she had been when they met into a hard-working monarch and a lover of nature's subtle splendors.

Aside from all that, the queen had continued to love her husband passionately. His death was devastating. And the fact that he had fallen ill while returning from a trip to Cambridge, where he had gone to express his moral outrage over their son Albert Edward's scandalous affair with an Irish actress, made the queen's sorrow even deeper. Ever after, she blamed Albert Edward (known as "Bertie," and later King Edward VII) for his father's death.

Victoria dressed in mourning black for the rest of her long life. During the first years after Albert's death, she withdrew entirely from the official and ceremonial appearances that were expected of the queen. Deeply depressed, she sought a change with a trip to Germany, the home of her Hanover ancestors (she was from the same family as England's German-born George I and George II). She included among her traveling retinue one particular servant from the royal summer place in Balmoral, the ever-reliable John Brown, whom she described as a combination "groom, footman, page, and maid." Brown also proved indispensable in keeping the queen from harm during two 1864 carriage accidents in Scotland. The following year, Victoria's doctor thought it a good idea that Victoria, still withdrawn from public life, pursue one of her favorite Balmoral activities—riding in her pony-cart—on a more regular basis, year-round as weather permitted. Brown, who had always led the pony and tended the cart on the summertime Highland outings, was brought down to Windsor Castle in England to do the same there.

Within a short time, Brown became Victoria's full-time personal attendant, outdoors and in. She created the post of

"Highland servant" for him, although he was with her everywhere from Aberdeenshire to London to the European continent. He reported directly to the queen, in her bedchamber. He sometimes spent hours closeted with her. He not only led her pony, he accompanied her on picnics—al fresco meals packed just for the two of them.

Other servants and members of the household quickly came to resent this roughhewn interloper, especially as the queen began to dispense orders to the rest of her palace staff through Brown, making him in effect her household manager.

Brown had an abrupt way of talking, whether he was addressing fellow servants or the queen's family. Author Christopher Hibbert, in a biography of Victoria, describes an occasion when Victoria sent Brown to issue a dinner invitation to household members who were assembled in another part of the palace. The invitation, delivered in Brown's distinctive style, was "All what's here dines with the queen."

Victoria also used Brown as a go-between with ministers and officials, as when she sent Brown to decline a request from the mayor of Portsmouth that she attend a function. The Highland servant came into the sitting room where the mayor waited, along with the queen's private secretary. "The queen says certainly not," was the extent of the message, delivered in his Highland burr.

Brown had first impressed Prince Albert and then Queen Victoria at Balmoral because he did not act deferentially toward them. He spoke his mind. This might be a dangerous practice for most servants, but somehow Brown had a confident air about him that made his blunt talk seem honest rather than disrespectful.

As Brown moved ever more freely among the queen's household and society, he never learned to show deference to those who were, by the conventions of English class and rank, his social betters. Under the queen's protection, he didn't need that skill. Brown once grew tired of listening to William Gladstone, the prime minister, and interrupted the Parliamentarian with "You've said enough." He reportedly addressed the queen as "woman," as when he admonished her to raise her chin so that he could fasten her bonnet, or when he disapproved of an article of clothing that she wore. No one else in the United Kingdom could have spoken to her so, probably not even Prince Albert when he was alive.

As the queen returned to public duties, she did so with the condition that Brown accompany her at all times, over the objections of government ministers. In palace matters, meanwhile, Brown's status continued to grow. He took first rights over royal hunting grounds and fishing spots, assuming precedence even over the queen's princely sons and official guests. Victoria banned smoking in her presence and prohibited it in almost every room, but Brown's foul-smelling pipe was exempted from the rule. She also ignored, and thus appeared to excuse, his excessive fondness for Scotch whiskey.

An amateur artist, the queen sketched several portraits of Brown. From well-known professionals, she commissioned portraits of him. She wrote him letters addressed to "dear friend" and on at least one occasion calling him "darling."

Around the royal household, other, less-favored servants began referring to the Highlander as "the royal stallion." The queen's daughters, although they also resented Brown, laughingly dismissed the rumors about a sexual affair. Between themselves, however, they referred to Brown as "Mama's lover." These were jokes, but rather dangerous ones, given the times.

Why did anyone care whether the queen was sleeping with a gillie? They were both single, after all. She was a widow, he a bachelor. Whose business was it if two consenting adults enjoyed each other's company—in a physical sense or not? The answer is that it was the business of everybody with a stake in the institution of the monarchy of the United Kingdom. That meant everyone from the Prince of Wales (Albert Edward, his mother's heir) to Conservative politicians to the royal gardeners.

Even in the twenty-first century, the tabloids would be all over a story about the queen's romance with a servant, especially that part about a secret marriage. Then, as now, it didn't have to be true to be published. And in the middle of the nineteenth century, the monarchy was hardly on firmer ground than it is today. During Victoria's reign, it had begun to occur to many in Britain that for the institution to endure, it needed popular support, which was in short supply. Royal prestige had suffered through the tenures of the Georges. The first two, born and raised as German princes, had despised everything English. Their English subjects had returned the sentiment.

The third George was a serious-minded sort who had patched things up to some degree by speaking English and by his dedication to government matters, but he lost the American colonies and then descended into madness. (See chapter 12.) Before losing his mind, George III sired a number of slacker sons who, as grown-up princes, did little besides sponge off the national treasury—or so the resentful English saw it. Two of those sons became British kings, the charming and brilliant but dissolute George IV (chapter 13) and the less than charming but more attentive William IV. Although both had fathered many bastards, neither had a direct legitimate heir. Upon William's death in 1837, the crown passed to his niece Victoria, then a petite eighteen-year-old. She was bright, strong-willed, and well intentioned, but at only five feet tall and with a girlish, bell-toned voice, she hardly radiated sovereign authority.

During the first decade of her rule, political unrest roiled through continental Europe, where revolutionary fervor then exploded into violence in several countries simultaneously in 1848. England felt the same forces that fed that violence—economic inequality, social resentment, a call for representative government. Many of Victoria's subjects questioned the worth of the monarchy. Many thought it had outlived its use-fulness.

To some extent, Prince Albert, although unpopular himself (another German interloper, the English thought), had before his death begun to repair the rift between queen and subjects, especially the middle class. A high-minded sort, he managed by his upright behavior and outspoken morality to position the royal family as an exemplar of proper British Christian behavior. This was a somewhat novel idea, one that would have been laughable under most previous kings and queens, but for Albert and Victoria—generally well-behaved and unquestionably mutually monogamous—it helped to restore a bit of respect for the monarchy, setting a moral tone for what would come to be called the Victorian Era. It was an era in which sexual intercourse was expected to take place exclusively within marriage. The Victorians were neither stupid nor naive, of course, but they believed that behaviors falling outside the bounds of common decency must be conducted with a certain discretion. It was simply polite. In the matter of Mr. Brown, Victoria gave the appearance of being indiscreet, even if she had nothing to be indiscreet about.

Rumors like those swirling around the queen's friendship with her favorite servant proved useful to critics of Victoria and also to critics of the monarchy in general. Newspaper and magazine cartoonists depicted Brown not as the power behind the throne, but as the man in front of it. Pamphleteers mocked the queen as "Mrs. Brown." Magazines wrote parodies in which palace life revolved completely around the whims of this kilt-wearing northerner.

If what appeared in print was scurrilous, then what was talked about over tea was surely more so. The politician Wilfred Scawen Blunt wrote in his diary (made public in the 1970s) about a secondhand report that Victoria and Brown, when at Balmoral, liked to retreat to a little house in the woods where his bedroom lay adjacent to hers, with a door in between. Blunt indirectly attributed this report to the sculptor Edgar Boehm, who had been commissioned by the queen to produce a bust of Brown. Boehm supposedly commented that the queen afforded "every conjugal privilege" to her personal servant. Blunt did not hear these things directly from Boehm, however, but from a noblewoman who said that she heard them from Boehm.

Those who knew Victoria well, including her private secretary, Henry Ponsonby, insisted that there was no substance to the rumors. They dismissed as unthinkable the idea that she would contract a secret marriage with Brown. Most historians since have agreed that the bond between queen and gillie was most likely one of profound mutual devotion, yet strictly platonic. Still, rumors continued to surface through the twentieth century and into the twenty-first. There are stories in which more than three hundred incriminating letters sent between the lovers surfaced after Victoria's death, only to be burned by her son Edward VII. How credible such stories are is difficult to say.

In the spring of 2003, the *British Diarist*, a quarterly magazine, published excerpts from the diary of Lewis Harcourt, again raising the issue of a secret marriage. Harcourt was the son of Sir William Harcourt, who held the post of home secretary when Gladstone was the prime minister of England. In 1885 Harcourt wrote about a deathbed confession, supposedly offered up by the Reverend Norman Macleod, who had been the queen's chaplain. By this account, Macleod regretted that he had presided over a secret ceremony in which Victoria and Brown had married.

Harcourt wrote in his diary that the source of this story, the Reverend Macleod's sister, was unlikely to have invented such a story about her own brother—a fact that made it somewhat believable to Harcourt that such a "disgraceful" wedding really had taken place. She did not tell the story directly to the diarist, however; Lewis Harcourt got the story from his father,

William, who said he got the story from Lady Ponsonby (the wife of private secretary Henry), who said she got it directly from Miss Macleod (who, to belabor a point, got it from her dying brother). This is hearsay upon hearsay upon hearsay, and thus inadmissible testimony—not just in a court of law but to any fair-minded truth seeker. Yet it's undeniably interesting.

Journalist Petronella Wyatt, writing in 2006 for the *Daily Mail*, a British newspaper, recalled hearing another account in which evidence of a secret marriage was found and promptly destroyed. The reporter wrote that she heard this from the Queen Mother (Elizabeth Bowes-Lyon, the widow of George VI and the mother of Elizabeth II), who was a friend of Wyatt's father. Once when the Queen Mum was over for dinner, she told the Wyatts that she had found papers in the royal archives supporting claims that Victoria and Brown had married. When Wyatt asked what she had done with the papers, her royal highness replied that she had burned them.

Mainstream historians, including most biographers of Queen Victoria, firmly believe such accounts to be, if not inventions, then distortions or misunderstandings. The accepted version of the truth is that Victoria came to care deeply for her burly guardian and that he, in his way, returned the sentiment, but that nothing of a sexual nature, nothing even of a romantic nature, ever took place between them. This is the way their relationship was portrayed, respectfully, in the touching 1997 movie *Mrs. Brown*, renamed *Her Majesty Mrs. Brown* when it was shown on the PBS program *Masterpiece Theatre*. (Judi Dench played Victoria.)

Yet questions persist. They must persist because of the obvious extremes of Victoria's fondness toward this man. The commissioned artworks—paintings, busts, a memorial statue, and memorial cairns—speak of something beyond what most people either then or now consider to be simple friendship. The depths of Victoria's grief when Brown died—a physical and emotional blow that temporarily rendered her unable to walk, suggests that she was connected to this man in a way beyond anything that the biographers have quite grasped. She wrote to her daughter, Princess Victoria of Hesse, about the constancy of missing him, about how his passing had taken all joy from her life. And the mementoes of Brown that she so specifically ordered be placed in her coffin, mirroring similar mementoes of Prince Albert, speak of utter devotion to Brown's memory.

If that isn't love, what is? As for what kind of love they shared, the answer may have died with the Victorian age.

To investigate further:

Arnstein, Walter L. *Queen Victoria*. New York: Palgrave Macmillan, 2007. This biography offers a complete and well-rounded look at the queen and her reign.

Auchincloss, Louis. *Persons of Consequence: Queen Victoria and Her Circle*. New York: Random House, 1979. A look at Victoria's rule through portraits of those close to her.

Benson, E. F. *Queen Victoria*. New York: Barnes & Noble, 1992. A reprint of a 1930 biography by a well-known novelist.

Hibbert, Christopher. *Queen Victoria: A Personal History*. Cambridge, MA: Basic Books, 2001. This well-written biography covers the queen's relationships with her family.

Lamont-Brown, Raymond. *John Brown: Queen Victoria's Highland Servant*. Stroud, Gloucestershire, UK: Sutton Publishing, 2002. A biographical portrait of the controversial servant.

Plunket, John. *Queen Victoria: The First Media Monarch*. New York: Oxford University Press, 2003. In an age of vigorous newspaper journalism, the queen experienced relentless scrutiny.

17

Did the Crown Prince Kill Himself, or Was He Murdered?

W hen word of the sudden death of the crown prince first reached Vienna on that gray January day in 1889, the report circulating the palace was that he had died of poisoning. It was potassium cyanide, administered by a young woman, Baroness Mary Vetsera.

But that wasn't true. Count Joseph Hoyos, the nobleman who supposedly first told the emperor it was death by poison, had that same morning let slip a different cause of death in a train station in nearby Baden. There, Hoyos said that the grand duke (as the crown prince was titled) had shot himself. He had not mentioned the baroness.

Yet the official announcement that was issued shortly there-after by the Hofburg, the royal palace of the Austro-Hungarian Empire, said something else entirely—that Grand Duke Rudolph, age thirty, had died of heart failure. Rudolph's father, Emperor Franz Joseph, personally wrote notes to the other

royal houses of Europe, informing kings and queens—including
Rudolph's father-in-law, the king of Belgium—of the tragic heart
attack that had taken the Hapsburg Dynasty heir. Again, no
mention of the young baroness.

The official story never stood a chance. Too many people
already knew it was a lie. Too many people had heard too many
conflicting versions.

On the morning of January 30, Hoyos and the grand duke's
chamberlain, Johann Loschek, had found Rudolph lying dead in
a mess of blood and gore. The scene was his bedroom at Mayerling, a royal hunting retreat about a half-hour southwest of
Vienna by train. Also in the room, naked and dead, lay
seventeen-year-old Mary Vetsera. Others at the retreat, guests
and servants alike, and people living nearby learned few details.
They saw and heard enough that morning and through the following day, however, to set tongues wagging.

As always, when someone—especially an official someone—
hides the truth, wild rumors fly. Some people in Vienna said that
Rudolph, known for his adulterous affairs with many women,
had seduced the wife of the Mayerling groundskeeper. The jealous groundskeeper had shot him.

That was before word spread about the nude teenager. She
was petite, with lustrous long brown hair, dark eyes, and an
upturned nose. Rumor shifted to speculation that Rudolph had
impregnated the pretty little baroness. Some said that Mary had
died in a botched abortion and Rudolph killed himself from
grief—or possibly shame. In a particularly romantic interpretation, he had killed her and himself in despair, because of the
impossibility, in Catholic Austria, of divorcing his wife, Grand
Duchess Stephanie, so that he could marry the one he truly
loved, Mary. Others with a lurid turn of mind said that the
young baroness had become hysterical over the pregnancy—or
over the impossibility of their ever marrying—and had cut off
Rudolph's penis, prompting him to kill her in rage and then,

devastated, to kill himself. A few theories clung to the idea that Mary, smitten with the dashing prince, had killed him when he tried to break off their affair and then had killed herself.

Yet Rudolph had powerful enemies, some of whom surely had wished him dead. He was, after all, next in line to wear the "dual crowns" of a mighty empire—the joined lands of Austria and Hungary, along with Poland, Croatia, parts of Italy and Romania, what would become Czechoslovakia (later the Czech Republic), and other areas. Furthermore, he was an intellectual and a political liberal. Unlike his father, an imperial absolutist, Rudolph aligned himself with the progressive movement within nineteenth-century social philosophy. He believed strongly in the rights of humankind and was sympathetic, at least to a degree, toward nationalistic (if not separatist) movements within the empire.

Rudolph also disliked and distrusted his cousin, the recently crowned Emperor (Kaiser) Wilhelm II of the powerful and belligerent German Empire. Rudolph considered Wilhelm a narrow-minded, dull-witted, backward-thinking dolt. While Wilhelm plotted violent conquest, Rudolph dreamed of a Europe at peace. He thought and had written about ways that such a thing might be achieved. There were certainly people among the powerful, in Vienna, Berlin, and elsewhere, who would have preferred that this idealist never come to power. Might someone—perhaps Wilhelm or even an official within Franz Joseph's inner circle—have ordered the grand duke killed?

The story that eventually prevailed said no. It was that Rudolph, frustrated at his political impotence under the regime of his conservative father, had decided that life was not worth living. Although a dedicated soldier and sportsman, the grand duke had also been an art lover with a romantic, perhaps even a melodramatic, streak. He drank heavily and used morphine, thus had become despondent and decided that his only escape from his intolerable existence lay in suicide. He had invited Mary, his latest mistress, to join him in a glorious death, and the naive girl had been so love-struck by the handsome, mustachioed royal that she had agreed. In the bedroom where Loschek and Hoyos found the bloody corpses, they also found a number of good-bye letters to loved ones, some apparently written by the grand duke and others by the baroness.

Even Emperor Franz Joseph gave up on the heart attack explanation and conceded that his son committed suicide. He appealed to Pope Leo XIII to allow a Catholic burial, which at that time was usually denied to one who had taken his own life. The court physicians who examined the body were instructed to testify, for this purpose, that there had been an abnormality of the brain resulting in insanity. Thus, the grand duke had not been responsible for his actions, and his death could not be interpreted as a willful suicide. At least one physician also referred to Mary Vetsera's death as suicide. In other words, like him, she took her own life with the service revolver that Loschek and Hoyos had found on a chair beside the grand duke's bloody bed.

But had she? Had either of them? As many historians have pointed out in looking back at the Mayerling incident, the mystery has never been solved because it was never properly investigated. The first impulse among the royal family and their servants was to cover up, dissemble, lie. Thus the conflicting stories and confusion.

Victor Wolfson, in his book *The Mayerling Murder*, assembled a narrative of what happened directly after the bodies were discovered, based on the memories of Loschek, taken down decades later, along with official police records and the memoirs of Countess Marie Larisch, Rudolph's cousin. Count Joseph Hoyos had immediately called court physician Hermann Weiderhofer to the scene, and Countess Larische's account was supposedly based on what Weiderhofer told her.

With minor differences, these sources related that Loschek had gathered up Mary's body and taken it to a nearby laundry closet, where he laid it atop a large wicker hamper. There it remained for a day, hidden under a sheet in an attempt to keep others who visited the scene from learning that she had been there and that she also had died. After Dr. Weiderhofer examined her body—using a billiard table in an adjoining room for the purpose—and attributed her death to a gunshot wound in the left temple, two of her uncles and another imperial physician were called from Vienna to take care of the body.

The emperor told Mary's uncles—Alexander Baltazzi and Count Georg Stockau—to remove the body in such a way that it appeared that Mary was still alive. The grief-stricken uncles dressed the corpse in Mary's silken underwear, a corset, stockings, petticoats, a smart olive green worsted suit (dress and matching jacket), a hat with a feather plume and a veil (the better to hide her shattered head), and fashionable boots. To comply with the emperor's order that she appear alive, they used a walking stick (or possibly a broomstick) tied to the back of her neck with a handkerchief to prop her head erect. Then, holding the dead girl—a child upon whom they had doted since her infancy—upright between them, they carried her out of the grand house and into a waiting carriage. They propped her corpse on the seat for the macabre ride to a nearby abbey. The burial was to be secret.

Emperor Franz Joseph could not convince the world that his son and heir had died from heart disease, but he did manage to quiet the story—at least, within the empire. Newspaper readers abroad—in Paris, London, and New York—learned the name of the dead girl and some of the less savory details about how the prince had died. Out of respect for the imperial family, newspapers in Vienna and even Budapest stepped more lightly. Within Austria-Hungary, most publishers refrained from printing the name Mary Vetsera.

It was only after the emperor died in 1916, in the middle of World War I, that journalists and scholars began to reexamine the case. Yet the story of the Mayerling incident, as it came to be called, changed little. Police records released after Franz Joseph's death included interviews with Rudolph's companions, stressing the grand duke's long-standing fascination with the subjects of death and suicide. His drinking and drug use emerged as major factors in an emotional decline. Austrian scholars such as Count Carl Lonyay studied the grand duke's correspondence, finding in them clues to his despondency.

Rudolph's historical portrait solidified as one of an heir tired of waiting for his crown. He was consumed with frustration and hopelessness—over his powerlessness, the lack of respect shown him by his hidebound father, imperial policies with which he disagreed, the state of Europe at large, and his loveless marriage to his wife, Stephanie. A police report revealed that he had earlier asked another mistress, the self-described "dancer" Mizzi Caspar, to die with him, but that she had made light of it, pretending it was a joke. Apparently, in the girl Mary Vetsera he found the suicide-pact partner he had earlier sought.

Most historians believe that Rudolph shot Mary. The location of the girl's entry wound as described by the imperial physicians, near the left temple, makes it highly improbable that the right-handed Mary wielded the weapon against herself. The doctors estimated her time of death as hours before the grand duke's. He must have then sat in the room with her body until he had gathered the resolve to kill himself.

Yet doubts may always linger. Twentieth-century author Wolfson, for example, argued that murder can't be ruled out. He looked at the same correspondence cited by suicide theorists and found evidence of a well-adjusted young man enjoying life. In Rudolph's letters to his wife, Stephanie, Wolfson saw indications of fond familiarity instead of a desperately strained relationship. One such letter, dated a few months before Rudolph's death, recounts routine events of the day, including minor annoyances, and closes with the grand duke telling his wife that he looks forward to a hot bath, in which he will smoke and sing. That, wrote Wolfson, gives evidence not of despair at the banality of his life, but of a zest for small enjoyments.

If Rudolph were demented by drug addiction—another argument in favor of suicide—then why, Wolfson asks, would he write to Stephanie about his misgivings over using morphine to treat a stubborn cough?

The suicide notes that the grand duke wrote to his mother and others close to him (although not to his father, the emperor) and that Mary wrote to her friends and relatives have been offered as proof that the lovers agreed to die together. Yet there are inconsistencies in the accounts of where Hoyos and Loschek found the letters, on the desk or in a drawer. Some accounts say that the letter to the grand duke's mother was in the room where he died; others say that it was left in his apartment in Vienna. Wolfson asked how Mary would have found time to compose the several letters that were reportedly found written in her hand, especially if she really had died hours before the grand duke did. Wolfson speculated that anyone staging a murder to look like suicide would take care to provide suicide notes, and he pointed out that the government in Berlin had in its employ experts in the art of forgery. He wondered that Loschek claimed not to have heard gunfire on the morning that the grand duke was supposed to have fired the fatal shot into his own head.

The author also questioned why the government banished Loschek, who had been Rudolph's faithful servant, from the empire after the incident. He wanted to know why Joseph Bratfisch, the grand duke's coachman, was offered a bribe to leave Austria-Hungary and why others who had been at Mayerling on January 30 were sworn to secrecy. He asked why the deceased's papers were confiscated and apparently destroyed. He speculated that Mizzi Caspar accepted a bribe to invent the story that Rudolph had invited her to die with him.

Furthermore, the author brought up a diary, which he attributed to the grand duke's personal secretary. It referred to a group of four unnamed Prussians—supposedly in Austria either to trap animals or to hunt for sport—who were staying at an inn near Mayerling just before the murders. The same four Prussians then showed up in the frigid pre-dawn darkness of the next morning, walking purposefully away from the royal retreat before the bodies were discovered. Could these men have been assassins in the pay of Berlin? Wolfson, who died in 1990, had no proof for any of his suspicions. In fact, several of his objections—the banishment of Loschek, for example—could be explained away by the emperor's desire to suppress the story. Nonetheless, the author raised interesting doubts.

Over the course of the twentieth century, some history-minded Austrians became positively obsessed with Baroness Mary Vetsera. Did she die for love? Was she the victim of an imperial cover-up devised to mask more than a grand duke's shame? According to Vienna journalist Georg Markus, at least one devotee regularly videotaped the girl's grave at Heile-genkreuz Abbey through the 1980s and into the 1990s.

In his book *Crime at Mayerling*, Markus recounts a story that he covered as a newspaper reporter in the 1990s, when another fanatic stole Mary's remains from her tomb in an attempt to find out how she really died. Linz businessman Helmut Flatzel-steiner approached Markus in 1992 to say that he had possession of the body, or what was left of it. Flatzelsteiner claimed that he had purchased the corpse from a pair of grave robbers who had taken it in hopes of finding valuables. He told Markus that he had arranged for a physician to examine the remains by telling the doctor that it was the skeleton of Flatzelsteiner's own grandmother.

Sure enough, Austrian police then found the sealed tomb empty. The story grew stranger. It turned out that Flatzelsteiner himself, obsessed with the story of Mayerling, had dug up the girl's coffin. His story about buying the body was a lie. To get at the coffin, he had used car jacks and a steel bar to pry up three heavy granite slabs from atop the tomb.

The skeleton was in reasonably good shape. Although most of the flesh had rotted away from the body, the clothing was intact. It was the same clothing that the girl's uncles had dressed her in to smuggle the body out of Mayerling more than a century earlier. Still attached to her skull was the long, abundant hair featured in every description of young Mary.

The peculiar episode provided an opportunity for forensic anthropologists to examine the girl's remains before they were re-interred. They reported that the skull was indeed damaged at the left temple. This confirmed that it was extremely unlikely that she shot herself. The damage was so extensive, however, that it was impossible to attribute her death to a gunshot and nothing else. She might have been beaten. Some Mary Vetsera devotees prefer to think that the baroness died not by consent, but as the result of a mad attack with a blunt instrument. Yet it's also possible that the cranium was damaged further after she died. Flatzelsteiner was not the first to exhume the body. Invading Russian soldiers desecrated her grave during World War II, pulling the original copper casket from the ground in a hunt for jewels. Austrian officials later put the remains in a second casket and reburied it, although perhaps not with the greatest care. Flatzelsteiner claimed that he found the bones in a jumble, not remotely in anatomical order.

The businessman, who managed to escape prosecution for disturbing Mary's grave (he did cover the costs of another new coffin, her third, and of re-interring her), then tried to convince Austrian authorities that they should next exhume the body of the grand duke. Even in that extremely unlikely event, there may be no evidence to prove exactly how he died. Those who have studied the issue most extensively (some of whose books are listed under "To investigate further" at the end of this chapter) find no reason to think it was not a suicide pact, and their shared opinion—barring dramatic evidence to the contrary—will stand.

Probably the best argument against murder is that Loschek and Hoyos both said, without contradiction from any other source, that they had to break down the bedroom door to discover the carnage. The door was locked from the inside.

Beyond the mystery of why and how Rudolph died, the Mayerling incident raises intriguing questions about the results of his death. Serious historians warn against playing "what if" with the past. But since this book is intended as an entertaining look at some of history's loose ends, it's permissible here to wonder whether Rudolph, had he lived, could have done anything to stop World War I. The world might be unimaginably different if he had.

Gavrilo Princip set off the war when he shot and killed Franz Ferdinand, the royal heir to the Austro-Hungarian Empire, on an early summer day in 1914. Yet Franz Ferdinand, the emperor's fifty-one-year-old nephew, never would have been in line for the crown if his cousin Rudolph had lived.

The war, or a war very like it, surely would have erupted without Princip, a short, skinny, nineteen-year-old Serbian terrorist. The fuel for an international conflagration was piled high, in the form of tense rivalries among European neighbors and powers tightly interlocked into reactive military alliances. At that moment in history, it was more than likely that if any two European nations went to war against each other—especially if one of them was Austria-Hungary—the entire continent would follow. Princip, one of many Bosnian Serbs enraged over the empire's 1908–1909 annexation of Bosnia, merely lit the match that day in Sarajevo.

The empire and its allies—Germany and the Ottoman Empire—lost the resulting war. Hungary, Czechoslovakia, and other nationalist entities pulled free of Austria, breaking apart the empire. Austria itself became a republic. The ancient Hapsburg Dynasty finally died. And in Germany, postwar resentments and privations built toward another world war, the one that started when Adolf Hitler—born the same year that Rudolph died and less than 170 miles away—invaded Poland in 1939.

Rudolph was interested in averting war. He probably would have opposed the empire's annexation of Bosnia or at least the sudden way it was announced. He certainly would have felt unease at the terms of the military alliance between Austria-Hungary and the German Empire as they stood in 1814. Yet when the war broke out, Rudolph's eighty-four-year-old father, Emperor Franz Joseph, still reigned.

For Rudolph to have made a difference, he would have needed to use the years between 1889 and 1914 wisely. Under one possible scenario, he could have built a progressive political base within the empire, one strong enough to exert pressure on Franz Joseph and perhaps moderate the emperor's absolutist and militaristic policies. Under another, the grand duke might have worked to establish a better relationship with his father, one that would have resulted in the elderly Franz Joseph coming to listen to his son and trust his advice. Given Rudolph's character—his womanizing and drinking—neither seems likely, although it's possible that he would have matured.

Barring those possibilities, the only difference might have been that Princip's bullet would have killed Rudolph instead of Rudolph's cousin Franz Ferdinand on that June day in 1914. And the world would have been much the same.

To investigate further:

Barkeley, Richard. *The Road to Mayerling: Life and Death of Crown Prince Rudolf of Austria.* London: Phoenix, 2003. A biographer examines Rudoph with the goal of explaining what happened at Mayerling in 1889 and why.

Crankshaw, Edward. *The Fall of the House of Habsburg.* New York: Penguin, 1983. The Mayerling incident is among several factors contributing to the end of a dynasty.

Judtman, Fritz. *Mayerling: The Facts behind the Legend.* Edinburgh: Harrap, 1971. The author revisits the scene of the crime with the aim of paring away legend.

Lonyay, Count Carl. *Rudolph: The Tragedy of Mayerling.* New York: Charles Scribner's Sons, 1949. This book focuses on the two deaths and their effect on the empire.

Markus, Georg. *Crime at Mayerling: The Life and Death of Mary Vetsera, with New Expert Opinions Following the Desecration of Her Grave.* Riverside, CA: Ariadne Press, 1995. A journalist interweaves the grave-robbery case with the story of the two deaths.

Morton, Frederic. *A Nervous Splendor: Vienna 1888–1889.* New York: Penguin, 1980. The author brilliantly depicts the few short but significant months leading up to the tragedy, with a cast of Viennese characters that includes Sigmund Freud, Johannes Brahms, Gustav Klimt, and more.

Palmer, Alan. *Twilight of the Habsburgs: The Life and Times of Emperor Francis Joseph.* New York: Atlantic Monthly Press, 1994. This biography covers the long life and long reign of the emperor that ended in World War I.

Wolfson, Victor. *The Mayerling Murder.* New York: Prentice-Hall, 1969. Wolfson attacks conventional depictions of Rudolph and challenges the assumption that the grand duke committed suicide.

18

Was Anna Anderson Russia's Anastasia?

On February 17, 1920, Berlin police fished a half-drowned young woman from the Landwehr Canal. She appeared to have jumped from a bridge in an attempt at suicide. Speaking in a peculiarly accented and ungrammatical German, she refused to tell them who she was or where she belonged. She said she had reasons for refusing. The police dubbed her Fräulein Unbekant—"Miss Unknown."

The woman seemed afraid of something, to the point of irrationality. Not knowing what else to do with her, authorities found a bed for her in an institution for the mentally ill. Doctors who examined Miss Unknown upon her admission to the asylum found evidence of trauma, including a creaselike scar behind her ear, consistent with a bullet wound, and a star-shaped scar indicating that her foot had been pierced through by a triangular-shaped spike of some sort—like a Russian bayonet. There were numerous other scars, indicative of many lacerations, and evidence of deep wounds to the chest and the arm, incompletely healed.

The young woman continued to withhold her name, explaining that she was afraid of persecution. She struggled against having her picture taken.

Almost two years later, Miss Unknown emerged from the asylum as the Grand Duchess Anastasia Romanov, the youngest daughter of the late Emperor Nicholas II of Russia. (The Russian title grand duchess is roughly equivalent to princess in the English tradition.) Although she went by other names, including Fräulein Annie, Anastasia Tchaikovsky, Anna Anderson, and, after marrying late in life, Anna Manahan, the woman maintained her royal identity until her death in 1984 in Charlottesville, Virginia. Her claim rested on the testimony of several people who had known the young Anastasia and said that they recognized this woman as the same. They testified that Anna knew details of palace life and the imperial family that no one else could know, things like pet names, servant's names, the location of rooms within the palace, and trivial childhood episodes. Physical evidence included congenital bunions (a condition called hallux vulgus) matching those of the grand duchess and a cauterized mole in the same position on one of her shoulders. An expert witness matched the structure of Anna's ear to that of Anastasia's on photographs. A handwriting expert said that Anna's hand was too similar to Anastasia's for them to be two separate people.

Could this really have been Anastasia? In a monster legal case that dragged on through appeals from 1938 to 1970, German courts ruled repeatedly that Anna and her supporters failed to establish her identity as such. Neither could opponents of her claim—exiled Russian nobles and their relatives in the royal families of Denmark and the United Kingdom—establish their counterclaim, that Anna was in reality a missing Polish factory worker.

Bolshevik secret police reportedly executed Nicholas II, his consort Empress Alexandra, and their children—four daughters and a son—along with three servants and the family doctor, in a hail of bullets in July 1918. The ad hoc firing squad was assembled in a small half-basement room of a house in Yekaterinburg where the family had been kept prisoner by the revolutionary government. Executioner Yakov Yurovsky, in a report that finally came to light in 1989, wrote that he personally killed Nicholas and his son Alexei, the thirteen-year-old heir to the crown, with bullets to the head as his subordinates fired at the others. At least one of the servants and some or all of the four grand duchesses—Olga, 22; Tatiana, 21; Maria, 19; and Anastasia, 17—survived the initial volley of shots. It was found later that the czar's daughters had sewn precious stones, including diamonds, into the seams of their dresses and in between layers of corsets, to keep the valuables from their jailers. The jewels deflected some of the bullets. Yurovsky wrote that he and his men then fired more shots at the survivors' heads and stabbed them with bayonets until they stopped moving and crying out.

After soldiers dragged the bodies from the house, Yurovsky ordered that gasoline be poured on them and set afire. He also had sulfuric acid poured on the bodies before they were thrown down a mineshaft. Worried that they would be too easy to find there, Yurovsky later ordered them removed from the mineshaft and buried in a pit some distance away.

By other accounts—some of them perhaps little more than rumor—at least one of the young grand duchesses was still alive as the bodies were being taken out of the house. Some residents of the area much later said that one or two of the bodies went missing and that soldiers scoured the area looking for them. Neighbors of the Ipatiev house, where the imperial family had been held and killed, said that searchers specifically sought seventeen-year-old Grand Duchess Anastasia.

Perhaps there was more than rumor to the reports. In 1965, Heinrich Kleinbetzl told a German court that a few hours after the executions, he saw Anastasia, severely injured but alive. Kleinbetzl had at the time lived in Yekaterinburg, where he was apprenticed to the tailor who mended uniforms for the soldiers guarding the imperial family. Kleinbetzl said that on the evening of the executions he had delivered some uniforms to the Ipatiev house, just across the street from the tailor's shop. While there, he was frightened by gunshots and screams. When he returned home later that evening, his landlady was bustling around, boiling water, and told him that he could not use his room that night.

Realizing that she could trust him, she explained that the Grand Duchess Anastasia was in his room, wounded and unconscious. He helped the landlady care for the girl, who was covered in blood, especially her lower body. Although he did not know the individual members of the imperial family, he recognized this person as one of the women he had seen strolling in the courtyard of the Ipatiev house when he made deliveries and pick-ups there. He said she cried out when they washed her bloody chin, which he thought must be broken. He said that although Red Guards came to the house, asking about Anastasia, they did not search the rooms. Three days later a different soldier, the one whom the landlady said had first brought her, came to get the girl.

Anna Anderson's compatible version of the story had come out in bits and pieces, many of them out of chronological order. Opponents cited her faulty memory as evidence that she was making up her history as she went along. Supporters argued that her lapses stemmed from emotional trauma and from physical damage to the brain—at the least, a severe concussion.

In 1921, Berlin police apprehended a woman named Clara Peuthert after a dispute with her neighbors in which she appeared unstable. They committed the eccentric Peuthert, fifty-one, to the asylum where Miss Unknown resided. The older woman was assigned to the same ward, where she became fascinated with the quiet young patient. Peuthert, a sometime seamstress who had lived in Russia, had seen pictures of the Russian imperial family in a magazine and became convinced that Miss Unknown, with her deep blue eyes and high forehead, resembled them. She became convinced that her fellow psychiatric patient was really the Grand Duchess Tatiana. When she said so, Miss Unknown pulled her blanket over her head and would not come out.

Peuthert, allowed to leave the asylum, found an exiled czarist officer in Berlin and told him what she suspected. Impressed by a meeting with the mysterious woman, he helped to bring Baroness Sophie Buxhoeveden, who had been a lady-in-waiting to Empress Alexandra, to the asylum to see what she thought. The meeting did not go well. Miss Unknown refused to leave her bed. The baroness came to the bedside, but Miss Unknown hid under the blanket. Finally, the baroness lost patience, yanked the young woman from the bed, and stood her up, immediately declaring that she was too short to be Tatiana.

"I never said I was Tatiana," Miss Unknown later explained, after Peuthert's royalist allies had begun to win her trust. Given a paper with the names of the grand duchesses upon it, and asked to indicate which of the names was not hers, she struck through Olga, Tatiana, and Maria, but not Anastasia.

Prodded, she told a disjointed story in which she remembered falling behind one of her sisters as the bullets rang out and smoke filled the little room at Ipatiev house. She recalled nothing further until she woke up in a farm cart, bouncing along a rutted dirt road in the company of a man who called himself Alexander Tchaikovsky. He said he had rescued her. She said that Alexander and his brother, sister, and mother nursed her many wounds as they traveled back roads out of Russia to Bucharest, Romania. There, to her horror, she discovered herself pregnant with Alexander's child. Apparently, he had raped her during the journey. She gave birth to a baby boy and then married Alexander—at least, she remembered a Catholic wedding mass. She said it was very strange to her, raised as she was in the Russian Orthodox Church. Shortly after that, a robber shot Alexander on a Bucharest street as Alexander was trying to sell some of the jewels that Anastasia had sewn into her clothes. Leaving her baby with her husband's sister and mother, Anastasia traveled with Alexander's brother, Serge, by train to Berlin to find her Aunt Irene (Princess Irene of Hesse and by Rhine, the sister of Empress Alexandra).

In Berlin, thinking Serge had left her or she had lost him, Anastasia set out on her own to her aunt's palace. Fearful that no one would know her or that her aunt would condemn her for having borne a child out of wedlock, she changed her mind and, in despair, jumped from the bridge into the canal.

Detractors later argued that there was no record of Tchaikovskys—neither an Alexander nor a Serge—among the secret police and the guards who carried out the executions. (Records from the revolutionary era were, however, somewhat less than systematically kept.) Those disputing Anastasia's royal identity also said that if she had found herself in Bucharest, she would have sought out Queen Marie of Romania, a cousin of both Emperor Nicholas and Empress Alexandra, rather than try to reach Princess Irene in Berlin.

Subsequent visits to Miss Unknown from people who knew the imperial family produced mixed results. Grand Duchess Olga Alexandrovna, the younger sister of Nicholas II, came in secret from Denmark to visit the young woman and seemed for some months convinced that she had seen her niece. She sent affectionate letters and gifts. Later, she changed her mind and denounced Anna, as Miss Unknown came to call herself. Pierre Gilliard, a former imperial tutor, also seemed to accept Anna as Anastasia before deciding she was a fraud.

Gilliard's wife, Alexandra Tegleva, had been Anastasia's nanny. She was convinced that Anna was the girl she had known. She even reported that Anna had asked her to apply perfume to her forehead, something young Anastasia used to request because she wanted "Shura" (a pet name for Tegleva) to smell like a flower. Other supporters included Gleb and Tatiana Botkin, children of the family doctor who had been executed with the imperial family. The Botkins had played with Anastasia when all three were children, and they steadfastly said they believed Anna to be their former playmate. Detractors have charged that Gleb Botkin, above all other Anna supporters, helped to perpetrate a fraud by feeding her bits of information about the royal household that only an intimate could have known.

Released from the asylum, Anna stayed first with a Russian émigré family but left them when she thought they were exploiting her. She often undermined her own case by eschewing attention. Her strange and inconsistent behavior, which appeared sometimes capricious and often paranoid, surely lost her some support. Princess Irene came to see her supposed niece but did not give her real name. When Anna saw the princess, she ran away. After seeing only a glimpse of Anna, Irene thought that it couldn't be Anastasia. Later, she admitted that she wasn't sure. Anna, when questioned by members of the royal family about her memories, sometimes clammed up, as if reluctant or unable to answer. Other times, she tried to change the subject or became suddenly emotionally overwrought. During her prolonged court case, Anna occasionally refused to speak to examiners or defied the judge.

Regardless of her true identity, the young woman whom visitors saw in the 1920s probably looked considerably different from the way she had looked before 1918. For one thing, a dentist at the asylum had pulled quite a few teeth, including front teeth, so the shape of her lower face had changed. For another, she contracted tuberculosis and lost a great deal of weight, at one point weighing only eight-five pounds. (Anastasia had been a plump teenager.)

Anna's use of languages has been cited by both supporters and opponents as evidence of her identity. She refused to speak Russian, saying it reminded her of those who killed her family. Detractors argued that she could not speak it. Yet when spoken to in Russian, she seemed to understand and replied appropriately in German. Also, when struggling to find a name for something in German, she sometimes blurted out the Russian word. A doctor attending Anna during a fever delirium reported that she spoke perfect English in her sleep. Late in life, Anna moved to the United States, where she seemed almost instantly fluent in the language. She also seemed to have a command of French and used it when on a trip to Paris. Yet during court proceedings, she refused to give evidence of her knowledge—or lack thereof—of these languages.

Opponents argued that Anastasia had never studied German and thus could not choose it as her primary language. Supporters in her court battle were able to produce lesson books of the Grand Duchess Anastasia, showing that she had not only studied German but had done better in that language than in Russian.

The court case was about money, as are so many legal matters and family disputes. Relatives of the imperial family had filed claims to the millions in the czar's bank accounts—particularly in the Bank of England. Anna's suit was filed to stop them. Her supporters said that the royals who denounced her as a fraud had financial reasons for doing so. Detractors said that it was Anna and her retinue who had their eye on financial gain.

There were also dynastic considerations. Although the return of a Russian monarchy was an impossibility during the long decades of the Soviet Union, there were those who took very seriously the question of who was the rightful successor to Nicholas II. If Anna had been Anastasia, then that successor might have been a poor Romanian who went by the name

Alexander Tchaikovsky after his late father—a dreadful thought to many among the royalists.

Although the German courts could not settle the issue of Anna's identity, science later—after Anna's death in 1984—seemed to do so. After publication of Yurovsky's report in 1989, two Russian history and mystery buffs followed its clues to find what they thought was the burial site of the royal family. Russian scientists followed up on their lead and found nine skeletons in a pit.

In the 1990s, scientists had new technology—DNA analysis—that they could use to establish, or at least narrow down, the identity of tissue. The Russian scientists brought in English molecular geneticists who were able to extract small amounts of DNA from the bone fragments. Then the researchers used a technique called polymerase chain reaction to amplify the DNA, exactly replicating its molecules to create a sample large enough to analyze. To find out whether these could be the bones of the imperial family, they first identified a gene that occurs in slightly different forms on the X and Y chromosomes. By this means, they showed that there had been four male bodies and five female bodies buried in the pit.

Next, they looked for similar patterns in regions of DNA called short tandem repeats. These showed that five of the sets of remains—one male and four female—belonged to people who were closely related.

By examining mitochondrial DNA, the stuff that comes not from the cell's nucleus, but from energy-producing organelles called mitochondria, the researchers were able to establish a mother-daughter link between the skeleton that appeared to be that of the empress and three of the other female skeletons. Mitochondrial DNA passes directly from women to their children and does not mix with the father's DNA. This kind of test also showed that the four related females—presumably the empress and three of the grand duchesses—were related to Prince

Philip, the Duke of Edinburgh and the consort of Queen Elizabeth II. The czarina had been Philip's great aunt.

Mitochondrial DNA from the male family member matched
that of two living relatives of Nicholas II, descendents of his
maternal grandmother.

The other skeletons, unrelated to those five, appeared to
belong to Dr. Yevgeny Botkin, the family physician, and attendants. None of the remains could have belonged to Alexander, the heir to the crown, and the body of one of the grand
duchesses was missing. Could this be support for Anna's claim?
It could, according to U.S. forensic scientists who became
involved in the identification process. They thought it likely
that the missing grand duchess was indeed Anastasia, based on
the fact that she was by far the shortest—probably only five
feet, two inches. None of the skeletons appeared to belong to a
woman that small. Also, none of the skeletons seemed to belong
to a female as young as seventeen. Russian forensic scientists disagreed. Based on an analysis of skull dimensions, they thought
the missing daughter must be Maria.

In 2004, a team of Stanford University researchers chal-
lenged the earlier results and issued a report based on further genetic testing. These scientists stated that the first DNA samples
had likely been contaminated and that the bones had not been
shown to belong to members of the Russian royal family. The
issue had not been solved conclusively by August 2007, when
Russian archeologists announced their discovery of two more
skeletons at a separate burial site near where the earlier remains
had been found. The bones appeared to belong to a boy of ten to
thirteen years of age and a young woman between eighteen and
twenty-three. Although the researchers suggested that these
newfound remains may have been those of the Grand Duke
Alexei and one of his sisters, the scientists cautioned that they
could not say for sure until extensive tests were completed. If all
four of the young female skeletons could be shown conclusively

to have been the grand duchesses, it would eliminate all doubt about their fates.

Anna's body had been cremated after her 1984 death, at her own request, so when researchers decided to compare the DNA from the Yekaterinburg skeletons with that of the putative Anastasia, they seemed to have hit a dead end. There was a chance, however, that Martha Jefferson Hospital, in Charlottesville, Virginia, might have kept a bit of tissue from an intestinal operation that Anna underwent there. In 1968, she had married John E. "Jack" Manahan of Charlottesville and lived the rest of her life with him there. At first, hospital officials were unable to find a tissue sample from Anna Manahan. Months later, however, the hospital came forward with a bit of intestine attributed to her.

A further bit of DNA showed up in a book that had belonged to Jack Manahan. After his death in 1990, a bookseller had purchased the contents of his private library. Between the pages of one book was an envelope labeled "Anastasia's hair." In it were a few strands of hair.

The hospital sent the intestinal tissue to British scientists who had worked on the DNA analysis of the Yekaterinburg remains. The bookseller gave the envelope to author Peter Kurth, who had written a biography of Anna. Kurth gave it to a BBC reporter, who then passed it on to the British lab. Neither the tissue nor the hair was shown to contain mitochondrial DNA that matched those of the female skeletons or that of Prince Philip. Instead, they were shown to match a DNA sample taken from Karl Maucher, whose grandmother was the sister of Franziska Schanzkowska, the missing factory worker from 1920.

For those who had argued that Anna Anderson was a fraud, the case was closed. The woman had been a brilliant actress who nearly pulled off the greatest scam of the twentieth century. Those who believed in Anna, however, have refused to accept the DNA results. They find it suspicious that at first there was no intestinal tissue and then later the hospital found some. They point out that there is no certain way to link the hairs in the envelope to the head of Anna Manahan. And even if those were Anna's hairs in the envelope in the book, what was the chain of custody between the bookstore and the lab? Couldn't the sample have been switched? They are distrustful of Prince Philip, whose uncle, Lord Louis Mountbatten, had been a major financial supporter of the legal team that was assembled to prove that Anna was really Franziska Schanzkowska.

Finally, they ask, how can the DNA evidence explain Anna's many scars, her cauterized mole, and the foot condition identically matching Anastasia's? How does it account for the fact that Franziska Schanzkowska was three inches taller than Anna and wore a larger shoe size?

It can't. But neither is there a way to go back in time and measure both Anna and Schanzkowska as they stood in 1920, or to find out whether Schanzkowska, like Anna and Anastasia, also suffered from hallux vulgus.

DNA technology is advancing all the time, and in fact, the techniques used to examine the intestinal tissue and the hair attributed to Anna Manahan are already considered primitive. But if any tissue or hair remained to be analyzed, would the results be completely different? It's unlikely.

Short of trickery, short of a conspiracy so intent on masking the truth that its operatives would switch tissue and hair samples, the DNA results must stand. The woman who called herself Anna Romanov Tchaikovsky Anderson Manahan was not Grand Duchess Anastasia. She was, however, fascinating. And she remains a mystery.

To investigate further:

Ferro, Marc. *Nicholas II: Last of the Tsars*. New York: Oxford University Press, 1993. This biography includes both the public and the private lives of the emperor and his family.

King, Greg, and Penny Wilson. *The Fate of the Romanovs*. New York: John Wiley & Sons, 2003. The authors reexamine events leading up to and surrounding the executions.

Kurth, Peter. *Anastasia: The Life of Anna Anderson*. New York: Pimlico, 1995. The author supports the claim that Anderson was the grand duchess.

———. *Tsar: The Lost World of Nicholas and Alexandra*. Boston: Little, Brown, 1995. This lushly illustrated, beautifully designed book evokes a bygone era and tells the story of the brutal murders that ended it.

Lovell, James Blair. *Anastasia: The Lost Princess*. Washington, DC: Regnery Gateway, 1991. The author argues that Anna Anderson was Anastasia, and that European royals conspired to deny her claim.

McGuire, Leslie. *Anastasia: Czarina or Fake? Opposing Viewpoints*. St. Paul, MN: Greenhaven Press, 1989. An accessible presentation of claims and counterclaims.

Petrov, Vadim, Igor Lysennho, and Georgy Egorov. *The Escape of Alexei, Son of Tsar Nicholas II: What Happened the Night the Romanov Family Was Executed*. New York: Harry N. Abrams, 1998. This book is not about Anastasia, but about a Russian man whom the author claims was really the grand duchess's little brother.

Radzinsky, Edvard. *The Last Tsar*. New York: Doubleday, 1992. A good biography of Nicholas.

19

Why Was Edward VIII So Crazy about Mrs. Simpson?

D id anybody ever—in 1936 or since—really believe in some magical romantic bond between Edward VIII of the United Kingdom and Wallis Warfield Simpson, the couple who became the Duke and Duchess of Windsor? The press gushed about a devotion so deep that the king would renounce his crown to marry his true love. *Time* magazine put Mrs. Simpson on the cover as its Woman of the Year (displacing that era's traditional Man of the Year title).

Okay, maybe the editors were justified in their choice. She had, after all, changed history. On December 10, 1936, less than a year into Edward's reign, he surrendered his titles as king of the United Kingdom of Great Britain and Ireland and of the British dominions and emperor of India. Edward VIII is the only British sovereign ever to renounce the crown voluntarily. His reason, as stated in a radio broadcast to the British people that evening: "I have found it impossible to carry on the heavy burden of responsibility and to discharge the duties of King as I would wish to do without the help and support of the woman I love." Younger brother George VI, his successor, created the title of Duke of Windsor for the retired king. After Mrs. Simpson's divorce came through, the duke made her his duchess, and they lived happily ever after, so to speak. Those with a fairytale mentality on either side of the Atlantic mooned over the middle-aged lovebirds. Yet most observers—those with a few cerebral cells to rub together—said, "Huh?"

Men could not help but notice that which would have been ungallant to mention. The object of the king's love was not possessed of an unearthly beauty. At age forty, her flower of youth was past, and it had never been the lushest of blossoms. The prominent nose, thin lips, jutting chin, broad shoulders, and flat chest did not make the woman ugly (really), but neither did those features add up to a paragon of feminine charm. It was hard to picture her as the irresistible object of royal desire.

Many women also found it hard to warm up to the meticulously dressed, severely coiffed heroine of this modern romance. Even those too high-minded to gossip could not avoid observing that the king was throwing away his crown for someone who was still married to another man, her second husband. (Her marital status stood as the main reason that the Church of England, the rest of the royal family, Parliament, and Stanley Baldwin, the prime minister of Great Britain, found Wallis Simpson unacceptable as a potential queen.) What, exactly, were this American divorcee's mysterious charms? What did she have that King Edward could not live without? How did she snare him?

The answer may lie in the respective lives and characters of both the king and Mrs. Simpson. Born in 1894, Edward was the oldest child of George, the Duke of York, who became George V in 1910. Edward's mother, Mary of Teck, was a model of royal propriety. Although both parents were affectionate toward their seven children, they spent little time with the tykes. By custom and preference, royals left the rearing of their offspring to servants. One nanny took a particular interest in the little King Edward-to-be, smothering him in cuddles but also physically abusing him with deliberate scratches and pinches. She became so jealous of the little boy's attentions that she found ways to keep him away from the duke and the duchess. When it was almost time to present the toddler to his parents, she regularly scratched and pinched him painfully. Crying and fussing, the prince was brought before his mama and papa. Dismayed by their little man's ill temper, they sent him immediately back to his nanny, which was precisely the result she had sought.

That was likely when the duke began to consider his eldest—always small for his age—something of a milksop. The boy's full name was Edward Albert Christian George Andrew Patrick David, and the family called him David. To his father, he became "poor David."

To toughen him up, the duke sent poor David to sea, making him a Royal Navy midshipman. The adolescent's older and bigger fellow trainees cared nothing for his princely rank. When they weren't teasing and mocking David, they beat him mercilessly.

In 1910, Edward's father became king. With that change, the son gained a great many hereditary titles, the most significant being Prince of Wales. As heir apparent, the young man came into his own, as it were. During World War I, he secured a position as a junior officer in the Grenadier Guards and sought a front-line assignment in France. Both Parliament and the king forbade it, but the prince defiantly threw himself into harm's way several times during the war. Never the sharpest sword among the royal armaments, he may have exhibited more stupidity than courage with his reckless exploits, but he was awarded the Iron Cross. More important is the fact that he won the respect and affection of the British people. During the 1920s and into the 1930s, the prince assumed greater royal duties. He visited poverty-stricken areas and even developed a program to ease unemployment.

His efforts—along with his trim, compact good looks and bearing—brought him a degree of adulation something like that later achieved by his great-nephew's wife, Princess Diana. Prince Edward enjoyed celebrity on the level of a matinee idol. He also began to live like a celebrity. Rather than hobnobbing exclusively with the nobility and the politicians, he began to rub shoulders with a wider circle of high-society types—nouveau riche businessmen, socialite hostesses—accepting their invitations and inviting them to his country house. As a celebrity among celebrities, he dallied with film actresses. Tellingly, however, his mistresses were exclusively married women.

Bessie Wallis Warfield, on the other hand, was born not into royalty but at a modest mountain retreat in Pennsylvania. Although her birthday is officially listed as July 9, 1896, biographers have pointed out that according to the U.S. Census of 1900, she was really born in 1895. Her parents were not married when the child came, a situation made all the more scandalous in the context of Baltimore society. Both Teakle Wallis Warfield, the father, and Alice Montague, the mother, came from prominent families in that city.

Teakle and Alice did marry, but he was very ill with tuberculosis and died not long afterward. Alice and little Wallis, as the child was called, lived with relatives or in modest rented apartments in Baltimore. There were holidays at the country places of wealthy cousins, and Wallis went to the best schools that her mother could afford, but surely it was painfully obvious to the girl that she and her mother were poor relations.

After coming out as a debutante, Wallis traveled to visit a cousin in Florida, where she met Winfield Spencer, a naval officer. They were married in 1916. According to her memoirs, she discovered on their wedding night that he was a heavy drinker given to violence. After five years of verbal and physical abuse that included beating her, tying her to the bed, and locking her in the bathroom, she left him in 1921 to rejoin her mother, then living in Washington, D.C.

A few years later, Spencer, now transferred to Hong Kong, wrote to ask for another chance, so Wallis sailed in 1924 to the Far East. The reconciliation failed, but rather than return immediately to the United States, Wallis went to Shanghai and then to Peking, enjoying several flings with gentlemen among the Western contingents there.

Back in the United States, Wallis filed for divorce and developed a friendship with a businessman, Earnest Simpson, who then asked her to marry him. Feeling a need for security, as she wrote to her mother, she consented. Joining Earnest in England, where he had been sent to manage his shipping firm's London office, she became Mrs. Simpson in 1928.

In London, the newlywed Simpsons socialized with American diplomats. Wallis found a friend in Consuelo "Connie" Thaw, the wife of the U.S. Embassy's first secretary. Consuelo had a sister, Thelma, who had married into English nobility and who was the current mistress of the Prince of Wales. Thelma, whose title was Viscountess Furness, helped Connie to draw the Simpsons into the circle of the prince's intimate friends. Mrs. Simpson became one of his favorite dinner guests. In early 1934, Thelma, just divorced from the viscount, decided to travel to the United States to visit another sister, her twin, Gloria Vanderbilt (the mother of the Gloria Vanderbilt of designer jeans fame). Thelma told Wallis that the "little man," as she called his royal highness, would be lost in her absence, and she asked Wallis to look after him. Wallis obliged. Oh, did she oblige.

By the time Thelma returned, less than three months later, Wallis had made herself the mistress of Fort Belvedere—not de jure but de facto. She may not yet have been the prince's mistress, not in a sexual sense. She continued living in London with Earnest, but Wallis was already running the prince's household as if she were a cross between his princess and his housekeeper. She drew up the daily menus, managed the staff, supervised decor, and negotiated guest lists. She also took the prince himself in hand. At a dinner party on the night of Thelma's return, he casually reached to pick up a lettuce leaf from his salad with his fingers. Wallis, seated beside him, slapped his hand and scolded him to watch his manners. He smiled. The guests gaped. No one had ever done that to the prince, at least not since he had reached adulthood. Shocked, Thelma gave Wallis a sharp look. Wallis returned it, coolly. Both women knew that the guard had changed.

From then on, the prince was ever more devoted to Wallis Simpson, a circumstance that only seemed to intensify after Edward's father died in January 1936, making Edward the king. Friends observed that he was smitten—beyond smitten, he was hypnotized, hooked. Acquaintances commented on how deeply in love he was, how much he needed her, how he could not stand to be parted from her. Few observers have said anything about Mrs. Simpson loving the king in return. It might be uncharitable to assume that she did not, although a secret British government file, released in 2003, revealed that even as the new king attempted to win government acceptance for a marriage to her, Mrs. Simpson was secretly seeing yet another man, a handsome Ford Motor Company salesman named Guy Trundle. The king had by this time cut all ties to his other lady friends. It is said that in every relationship there is an adored and an adorer. In this one, Edward was the adorer. And here comes that question again: why?

Some biographers have asserted that Wallis Simpson offered the prince sexual delights beyond anything he had previously experienced, that she possessed special knowledge of erotic techniques that she had picked up during her stay in China.

Writer Charles Higham cites an elusive intelligence dossier, sup-posedly compiled by British spies during the 1936 abdication crisis, stating that the then Mrs. Spencer had learned the erotic art of Fang Chung in a Hong Kong brothel. A massage-relaxation technique, it involves stimulating nerve centers to heighten sex-ual awareness. Higham cites unnamed witnesses who claimed to have seen this secret file. If the file ever existed, however, it has not yet surfaced.

Biographer Michael Bloch speculates that whatever Mrs. Simpson's special sexual skills entailed, they were made nec-essary because she was physically incapable of standard sexual intercourse. Based on little more than hearsay and the slightly masculine aspects of her angular, slim-hipped figure, he puts forward the idea that she had been of indeterminate gender at birth but had been raised female. He makes much of a quote by British writer James Pope-Hennessy: "I should classify her as an American woman par excellence, were it not for the suspicion that she is not a woman at all." This line of thought can lead to the conclusion that what the king was looking for was someone who could satisfy latent homosexual urges while allowing him the illusion that he was wholly heterosexual.

Another, less lurid theory about what set this woman apart—what made the new king insist on marrying her, even after he knew that it meant he could no longer be king—is that she ful-filled emotional needs, rather than mere sexual impulses. There is a story, possibly apocryphal, that when they first met, the then prince asked Mrs. Simpson whether she missed American-style central heating, which was then rare in England. She replied, "You disappoint me, sir," admonishing him for asking such a clichéd question. It was the icebreaker question that every British man in the 1930s seemed to ask every Ameri-can woman in London. Whether that exchange happened or not, it illustrates the perception that Wallis did not treat her royal admirer with deference. There is the famous slap on the hand, for instance. Rather than angering him, it amused him.

In public, everyone was to address the prince as "sir." That had included his previous mistresses. Wallis called him David, his private name among family and close friends, and she sometimes addressed him familiarly in less-than-private situations. She also picked up from Thelma Furness the habit of referring to Edward in the third person as "the little man." Unlike Thelma, she sometimes let him hear her saying it.

In short, Wallis took charge, both of the prince's household and of his person. She bossed him around, and he loved it. He loved her for it. Perhaps there was a need in him to be pinched—if not literally, then figuratively—a craving ingrained by that abusive-smothering nanny when he was a toddler. Or perhaps he simply found it intoxicating to be with a woman who pampered him without fawning over him. She gave him relief from that gnawing doubt that people liked him, that women paid him attention solely because he was a prince.

Any of the previous theories suggests that Wallis happened to possess qualities—acquired skills or innate traits—that somehow met Edward's needs, needs that he hadn't even known were there. In other words, their meeting was serendipity, their love affair inevitable. When Wallis, by pure chance, came into his life, Edward suddenly felt completed. American writer William A. Cohen disagrees. The writer, who specializes in motivational topics for business leaders, says that Wallis had a plan, which she had confessed to an old schoolmate from Baltimore. (Such second-person testimony would not be admissible in a court of law, but it often serves historical speculations.)

Cohen, in his book *The Art of the Strategist*, describes Wallis's goals as, "Get to England. Meet the prince. Get him to fall in love with her. Divorce her husband. Marry the prince." In Cohen's language, this means that Wallis committed herself to a clear objective. She positioned herself within the prince's social circle, seized the initiative when opportunity arose (the absence of his mistress), made herself indispensable by taking over management of his household and life, and employed the element of surprise by treating him with such direct familiarity. These and other aspects of the romance demonstrate, in Cohen's view, a conscious use of universal strategic principles.

To Cohen, such principles are like "the force" in the *Star Wars* movies. They can be employed for good or for evil. He characterizes Wallis Warfield Simpson as a denizen of the dark side.

If so, she may have inadvertently worked good, rather than evil, with her carefully laid plan. Because of her, Edward VIII gave up his crown. When World War II broke out less than three years later, George V rather than Edward VIII was on the throne. This was significant because Edward—who was known for spouting casually racist comments—admired Adolf Hitler and his Nazi philosophy. As Duke and Duchess of Windsor in 1937, he and Wallis visited Germany as personal guests of der Fuehrer. For the United Kingdom to have had a Nazi sympathizer as king when Hitler invaded Poland would have been awkward, to say the least.

It is not clear that Mrs. Simpson was quite the calculating strategic engineer whom Cohen describes. Most likely, her conquest of the prince involved a combination of factors, among them a certain natural charm. He was not the first man, not by quite a few, who had found this woman fascinating. She may not have photographed well at age forty, but there was clearly a charm about her for those who met her face-to-face. As for the sexual business, the theories seem rather a stretch. Sex is an important part of romantic relationships but seldom the most important part. It hardly seems conceivable that a king would abdicate just so he could marry the girl who gave him the best roll in the hay—especially when he could have kept her as his mistress.

Wallis had not been above using her charms, subtle as they were, to advance her status in life. The marriage to Earnest Simpson seems little more than that. Having grown up poor, having felt inferior among her Baltimore society kin, she may have seen Edward's initial fondness for her as an unparalleled chance. He had what she wanted—great wealth and tremendous social status. She decided to get it.

Cohen is certainly right that she knew how to exploit an opportunity. She probably also possessed a talent for reading a man's character, intuitively realizing what he needed and, if she so chose, supplying it. Ultimately, that is the likeliest solution to the riddle of how she so captivated him. Edward was a needy man. Wallis took the trouble to understand what he needed. Then, she supplied it.

To investigate further:

Birmingham, Stephen. *Duchess: The Story of Wallis Warfield Windsor*. Boston: Little, Brown & Co., 1981. This biography tells the duchess's story from her humble Baltimore childhood.

Bloch, Michael. *The Duchess of Windsor*. New York: St. Martin's Press, 1996. Bloch delves into Wallis Warfield's early life and first marriage, with considerable speculation about her sexuality and her experiences before she met Prince Edward.

Higham, Charles. *The Duchess of Windsor: The Secret Life*. New York: John Wiley & Sons, 2004. The author, a show-business biographer, stretches credulity as he chases wild rumors, including some about the duchess's supposed adventures in international espionage.

McLeod, Kirsty. *Battle Royal: Edward VIII and George VI—Brother Against Brother*. London: Constable & Robinson, 2000. This book blames George V, a bullying father, and his wife, Queen Mary, an inattentive mother, for emotionally scarring their sons and setting the stage for lifelong sibling rivalry.

King, Greg. *The Duchess of Windsor: The Uncommon Life of Wallis Simpson*. New York: Citadel, 2003. The author's extensive and meticulous research has yielded a well-rounded, balanced, and surprisingly sympathetic portrait of the duchess.

Williams, Susan. *The People's King: The True Story of the Abdication*. New York: Palgrave Macmillan, 2004. Williams, a University of London historian, charges that Stanley Baldwin, the prime minister, and his political allies forced Edward VIII to abdicate.

Wilson, Christopher. *Dancing with the Devil: The Windsors and Jimmy Donahue*. New York: HarperCollins, 2000. Wilson, a former British newspaper reporter writes that the Duchess had a sexual affair with the American department store heir Jimmy Donahue, a notorious gay playboy.

Windsor, HRH Duke of. *A King's Story: The Memoirs of the Duke of Windsor*. London: Trafalgar Square, 1998. The duke's memoir puts his life and his wife in the best possible light.

Windsor, Wallis Warfield. *Wallis and Edward: Letters, 1931–1937*. New York: Avon, 1988. Their correspondence shows the deep affection between the lovers.

20

Did Secret Agents Assassinate Princess Diana?

S hape-changing reptile space-travelers from another dimension murdered Princess Diana. At least, that's one theory out of many that have tried to explain her death. The official version of what caused the 1997 car crash that killed the United Kingdom's most popular royal is somewhat less sensational.

Diana, the Princess of Wales, died from injuries suffered when the car in which she was a passenger collided with a concrete pillar in a Paris tunnel. Initial investigations of the crash focused on a pack of photographers who had followed the black Mercedes 280 S sedan carrying the thirty-six-year-old princess and her forty-two-year-old companion, Dodi al-Fayed, from the Hotel Ritz, where the couple had dined. Police and the public assumed that the photographers, by chasing and harassing the occupants of the Mercedes, had caused the crash. There was also a good deal of disgust over the behavior of those paparazzi who snapped pictures of the injured princess at the crash site.

An official French inquiry into the matter, however, absolved the photographers of blame. After two years of investigation, French officials reported that Henri Paul, the man who was driving, was drunk. His blood alcohol level was between 0.173 and 0.187 percent, more than three times the legal limit in France. He had also taken a prescription drug that is not supposed to be combined with alcohol. He should not have been driving at all, let alone operating a vehicle with which he was unaccustomed at high speeds. The crash that killed Diana, Dodi, and Paul could have been prevented.

Paul, who was head of security at the Ritz, was off duty on the night of August 30 when Dodi al-Fayed had him called back to work to serve as chauffeur—a job for which Paul was not licensed. Dodi liked and trusted Paul and wanted to use him in an attempt to fool the paparazzi who were gathered around the front of the hotel. Disorderly photographers had earlier in the evening prevented Diana and Dodi from eating at the restaurant they had planned on. They diverted to the Ritz, which is owned by Dodi's father and where there were security personnel to keep the paparazzi at bay.

Later that night, Dodi wanted to go back to his apartment, but he didn't want the photographers to follow. He decided to try to fool them into trailing his regular limousine, driven by his regular driver, while he and Diana slipped out the back way into another car driven by Paul. It didn't work. The paparazzi caught on and followed the second car. Paul drove fast to outrace them, too fast.

An official British investigation belatedly followed the French inquiry. This one took three years, but when lead investigator Lord John Stevens—the former head of London's Metropolitan Police—announced its conclusions in December 2006, they matched those of the French investigators. Paul had been drunk. The British investigators took pains to match the blood taken from Paul's body after the crash with other samples of Paul's DNA to eliminate the chance that the blood had been switched—either by accident or deliberately. The investigative report stated with certainty that the blood was Paul's and that he had been inebriated, at a level suggesting that he had around ten drinks before sliding behind the wheel of the big Mercedes. "Our conclusion is that, on all the evidence available at this time, there was no conspiracy to murder any of the occupants of the car," Lord Stevens said. "This was a tragic accident."

A formal coroner's inquest followed the British inquiry, nearly a decade after the events in question. Yet none of these proceedings has dispelled or is likely to dispel the rumors and the conspiracy theories—some considerably more believable than the alien reptile hypothesis—that surround the crash. Many people, notably the father of Dodi al-Fayed, refuse to believe that the deaths of his son and the princess were accidental. Mohamed al-Fayed, a wealthy Egyptian businessman and a long-time U.K. resident, has charged publicly that agents working for the British government arranged the fatal crash. He charges that Prince Philip, the Duke of Edinburgh, ordered the operation to prevent Diana, the ex-wife of Prince Charles and the mother of Prince William, from marrying Dodi, an Egyptian Muslim, and bearing his child. Philip, the husband of Queen Elizabeth II, is the father of Charles, the heir to the British crown. He is also known to dislike Mohamed al-Fayed.

Fayed claims that his son and the princess were deeply in love and that they were to be married. He says that the racist British establishment could not bear the thought of William, the eventual heir to the crown, having an Arab half-brother, and the political ramifications of such a link. Rumors that circulated in the press during the days and weeks following Diana's death said that she had been pregnant by Dodi. If that were true, and if al-Fayed was correct about the British establishment, would such a pregnancy be a motive for killing her? Perhaps, but the doctors who examined Diana after her death said categorically that she was not pregnant. Close friends whom she had talked to just days before she died said that although she was fond of Dodi, she was not in love with him and had no desire to marry him. The British report reflected this, concluding that the couple was not altar-bound.

Al-Fayed denounced Lord Stevens as "a mental case" and "a tool for the establishment and the royal family." He believes the report is a cover-up, intended to keep the real story hidden. In that, he has company.

Unlike government investigators, conspiracy theorists tend to move quickly and recklessly. Well before either of the official investigations began—in fact, on the very morning of the crash—rumors about what "really" happened began to circulate on the Internet. Bloggers speculated that the smash-up was not accidental and that the beautiful princess, beloved by admirers around the world, was murdered. Over the years that the French and British investigators proceeded with methodical care, some of the more colorful conspiracy theories found their way into books such as author David Icke's *The Greatest Secret*.

A former professional soccer player who possibly headed the ball a few too many times, Icke believes that the 1997 crash in the Paris tunnel was planned long in advance, probably since Lady Diana Spencer's birth in 1961. It was a ritual murder, he argues, plotted and set into motion by a clandestine international organization of reptiles that masquerade as human beings to control the world. Apparently serious, Icke also attributes the murder of John F. Kennedy, among many other history-shaping events, to these lizards, which include the world's most powerful political leaders. When disguised as humans, they go by names that include Bush and Clinton.

Not as outlandish as Icke's scenario, but still pretty far out is the one that authors Jon King and John Beveridge present in their book *Princess Diana: The Hidden Evidence.* Perhaps hoping to ride the coattails of the best-selling novel *The Da Vinci Code*, the authors argue that Diana was descended from the Merovingian dynasty—a family that from the late fifth to the mid-eighth century ruled much of what later became France. This is the noble family that *Da Vinci Code* author Dan Brown depicts as direct descendents of a union between Jesus of Nazareth and Mary Magdalene. That heritage, channeled through the House of Stuart, a family of Scottish kings, from 1371 and English royalty between 1603 and 1714, apparently made Diana a threat to the House of Windsor, her ex-husband's clan. Conceivably, she could have somehow arranged for the crown to bypass Charles and go directly to their son William—who through her is also descended from Stuarts, Merovingians, and Jesus himself. The Windsors, in league with an international secret Masonic society, decided that she must be eliminated, and they employed Britain's foreign intelligence agency MI6, along with the U.S. Central Intelligence Agency, to accomplish the job.

King and Beveridge are far more compelling in the parts of their book that describe the activities of government spies and private security firms that the authors say are hired by governments to carry out covert operations, especially murders, that cannot be traced back to their instigators. The book describes devices by which a spy can take over the controls of someone else's vehicle. They describe in detail the murder of a British military officer that they say was carried out with one of these devices to disguise his death as an accident. They include an account of what they believe was a failed attempt to kill Camilla Parker-Bowles in a similar collision. Mrs. Parker-Bowles, long a special friend of Prince Charles and a major factor in his divorce from Diana, later became Charles's second wife.

Along with other conspiracy theorists, the authors ask why security cameras mounted along the approach to the Pont de L'Alma tunnel and inside the tunnel itself were not running the night and the early morning of the crash. French authorities have attributed the lapse to a malfunction of the system, a power outage.

The authors say that just after midnight on August 31, the Mercedes driven by Henri Paul neared the tunnel entrance with a motorcycle carrying two people following closely behind. The motorcycle had tailed the car from the hotel. Suddenly, the bike pulled alongside the sedan and passed it. The person on the back of the motorcycle aimed a device at the Mercedes's windshield. This device is described as an antipersonnel flashlight developed for use by U.S. special forces. It emits a burst of light so powerfully concentrated that it not only blinds its target but also disrupts his nervous system.

At the mouth of the tunnel, a white Fiat Uno, a small coupe, slowed just ahead of the Mercedes and veered toward it, forcing Paul to swerve. The Mercedes clipped the left rear of the Fiat, breaking the taillight cover. Paul, incapacitated by the light assault, pulled so sharply to the left that he was headed toward the row of pillars in the center of the tunnel. He overcorrected, sideswiping the Fiat, which the authors say was specially weighted for use in this operation. He overcorrected again, fatally this time.

In this scenario, the agents in the Fiat stopped, checked to make sure that Diana was mortally injured, then injected the dying Paul with a cocktail of drugs and alcohol so that the blame for the "accident" would fall to him. The motorcycle, the Fiat, and another car that some witnesses say they saw emerging from the tunnel then disappeared so thoroughly that French police never found them.

King and Beveridge charge that British agents used just such tactics to cause fatal accidents in Northern Ireland, and that the crash in the Paris tunnel was virtually identical to a plan drawn up, but never carried out, for the assassination of Serbian president Slobodan Milosevic.

Both the French and the British inquiries looked into the possibility that the Fiat in question was one that belonged to photographer James Andanson, who had been among the paparazzi shooting pictures of Diana and Dodi earlier that summer. Andanson died in 2000. Al-Fayed has charged that Andanson was an agent for MI6. The agency has denied it. Some conspiracy theorists think that Andanson's death, although ruled a suicide by French police, could have been a murder to shut him up. Al-Fayed has speculated that Andanson killed himself out of remorse over the role he played in the crash.

Paint scrapings found on the Mercedes in which Diana died confirm that it hit a white Fiat before it hit the pillar, but investigators say the paint was incompatible with that on Andanson's car. Furthermore, witnesses who saw a Fiat approaching the tunnel just before the crash describe it as old and in poor condition, driven slowly and erratically by a Mediterranean-looking man, and with a large dog in the back seat. Andanson did not fit the description, and although he owned a dog, he was never known to take it with him in the car. And why would anyone involved in deliberately setting up a fatal collision for MI6 have his dog with him?

Those who think Diana was murdered have pointed out that her ambulance traveled extremely slowly on its way to Pitié-Salpêtrière Hospital, where she died. It also made stops. They have questioned why she was taken to that particular hospital when there were two others closer to the accident scene. French authorities have explained that their ambulance service, unlike those in the United States and Britain, is set up to act as an emergency room on wheels. Within the large ambulance, medical technicians were working to stabilize the princess's condition and the vehicle stopped more than once while they were trying to keep her heart beating. This tactic failed, because of undetected internal bleeding that could have been stopped only with surgery. As for the choice of hospital, Pitié-Salpêtrière was apparently the officially designated destination for high-priority cases on that particular early morning,

All assassination theories depend on the assumption that someone had something to gain by killing Diana—that someone either hated or feared her enough to hatch an elaborate plan. Would that someone be a member of the British royal family? The princess, whose marriage to Prince Charles had fallen apart spectacularly amid embarrassing revelations of his infidelity and hers, had been a painful thorn in the side of the monarchy. Rumor had it that after Charles and Diana separated in 1992, Queen Elizabeth II forbade the mention of her daughter-in-law's name within royal earshot. According to several writers who specialize in the affairs of the Windsor-Mountbatten family, Charles's father, Prince Philip, disliked Diana thoroughly. *Hate* may not be too strong a word.

Diana had breeched strict, if unspoken, rules of royalty by airing the family's dirty linen in public. She had refused to subordinate her own needs to those of the prince. Aside from a general incompatibility between the two partners, their marriage was doomed by Diana's unwillingness, or inability, to overlook her husband's preference for his mistress and country-house neighbor, Mrs. Camilla Parker-Bowles.

Herself the product of a painfully broken marriage, Diana was by many accounts insecure, needy, demanding, and mercurial in her friendships and loyalties. She was also smart and, on occasion, spiteful. The princess was almost precisely the opposite of what she appeared to be when Charles asked her to marry him. At their televised state wedding in 1981, many millions of viewers worldwide had seen a demure young thing of barely twenty—shy, overawed, and somewhat awkward. The mature Diana was anything but. With photogenic looks, a flair for fashion, and a rapidly acquired media savvy far beyond that of any other member of the royal family, soon after the ceremony she began to upstage her husband at public appearances. It did not take her long, either, to upstage his mother, the queen. Diana made it look effortless.

The more unhappy Diana became in her marriage, it seems, the more she took pleasure in presenting herself to the world as a new kind of royal—caring where Charles and his kin appeared disengaged, warm in contrast to their chilly correctness, as beautifully graceful and modern as they were horse-faced, stiff, and old-fashioned.

It helped, of course, that Diana really embodied a number of the qualities she presented in her public self. Her willingness to embrace, sometimes literally, people who were poor, dispossessed, even diseased, may have been played to the camera, but that did not negate the genuine care she felt for her charitable causes.

A thread of some conspiracy theories regarding Diana's death is that the military-industrial establishment feared Diana's public campaign for a worldwide ban on landmines, a cause to which she had devoted herself after her 1996 divorce from the prince. As this line of thinking goes, arms manufacturers feared that Diana's popularity would call too much attention to the evil explosives, leading to a ban that would cost them profits. Also in this vein, theorists charge that wealthy British and American investors feared that Diana would expose their stake in the international arms trade. So they took steps to silence her.

Diana herself apparently believed in conspiracy theories. She also exhibited a tendency toward paranoia. Author Penny Junor, an authority on Britain's royals, has written that servants and friends sometimes found themselves bewildered and hurt by Diana's accusations of disloyalty. According to Simone Simmons, the "spiritual healer" who penned a 2005 book about her supposedly close friendship with the late princess, Diana was convinced that Princess Grace of Monaco had been murdered to keep her from announcing plans to divorce Prince

Rainier. More to the point, Diana allegedly believed that she would be the target of a similar assassination attempt.

In a letter that Diana wrote to her butler, Paul Burrell, she predicted a staged accident aimed at killing her. Burrell said that the princess wrote the letter ten months before the crash in the Pont de L'Alma tunnel. Published in the *Daily Mirror* in 2003, the letter specifically mentioned an automobile crash and suggested that the brakes would be tampered with.

Some, including Simmons, have said that it was Charles whom Diana feared because her death would free him, under Church of England law, to remarry. The Anglican Church does not recognize divorce, as such. Thus, Charles and Diana were still married in the eyes of the church until her death. Although Charles could have married his longtime love, Mrs. Parker-Bowles, he might have sparked a constitutional crisis by doing so while Diana still lived, especially when it came time for him to ascend to the throne. The king is officially the head of the English church. With Diana dead, this barrier was removed. After a decent interval, Charles and Camilla did in fact marry in 2005.

Other theorists, such as Peter Hounam and Derek McAdam in their 1998 book *Who Killed Diana?* suggest that it would not have taken a direct order from any member of the royal family to set in action a plan to take Diana's life. They cite the example of Henry II, who in 1170 famously groused, "Will no one rid me of this turbulent priest?" He had not assigned assassins, yet soldiers took his remark as license to murder the insubordinate Archbishop of Canterbury, Thomas à Becket. Such an utterance made about Diana in 1997, the authors speculate, could also have set off a tragic and murderous chain of events.

There was a fourth person in the Mercedes when it crashed. Trevor Rees-Jones, one of the princess's bodyguards, was in the front passenger seat. He suffered a severe head injury and such extensive damage to his face that a plastic surgeon had to rebuild a visage for him. Yet he survived and recovered. As often happens in cases of extreme trauma, Rees-Jones remembers nothing of the crash. His memory of anything after leaving the hotel a bit before midnight is gone. Yet at least one memory from before leaving the hotel is telling. In his book *Bodyguard Story*, Rees-Jones writes of Henri Paul in the bar of the Ritz, waiting for the princess and Dodi to go. Paul was drinking glasses of a yellowish-white liquid, and the bodyguard remembers him making some joke about pineapple juice. Rees-Jones didn't get the joke. He thought, in fact, that the stuff in Paul's glass *was* fruit juice.

Sadly, it was pastis, a potent French liqueur. It is flavored with star anise, which in French is *anis*. French for "pineapple" is *ananas*. Paul was making a pun.

Was Diana murdered? It is possible, if unlikely. The problem with proving anything one way or another is that the chief investigators thus far have been the French authorities, followed by the British authorities. If indeed there was a high-level conspiracy to hush up whatever happened, and especially if secret government agents were involved, these authorities might well have conflicts of interest. They might be charged with obscuring, rather than uncovering, the truth. Diana died not long before the beginning of the twenty-first century, a cynical age in which public trust in government institutions is at something less than a high point. Doubts may always linger.

The problem with most conspiracy theories is that they assume that a group of human beings is capable of keeping a secret. This is not usually a reliable assumption. Yet spies are trained to keep secrets.

Perhaps the best reason for believing that the crash was an accident is that there's little doubt that Paul was drinking through the evening before it happened. His acquaintances remember him drinking at the Ritz that afternoon as he got off work. Others report him drinking in a bar when he got the phone

call asking him to come back to the hotel. And then there was
his anise-pineapple joke just before the fatal ride. How could
secret agents have arranged for him to go bar hopping? How
could they even know that Dodi al-Fayed would call in the security chief at the last minute and make him a substitute driver?
They couldn't—unless, of course, they were reptile space aliens
from another dimension. Those lizard guys have been known to
time travel.

To investigate further:

Berry, Wendy. *The Housekeeper's Diary: Charles and Diana before the
Breakup*. New York: Barricade Books, 1995. This engaging downstairs
view of Charles and Diana's daily life provides insights into the royal
couple's incompatibility.

Daymon, Joy Jones. *Princess Diana: The Lamb to the Slaughter*. San Jose,
CA: Writers Club Press, 2002. The author's case for murder is based
on unanswered questions and much speculation.

Dempster, Nigel, and Peter Evans. *Behind Palace Doors: Marriage and
Divorce in the House of Windsor*. New York: G. P. Putnam's Sons, 1993.
An anecdote-filled account of the marriage of Diana and Charles, portrayed in the context of the poisoned relationships that marked their
respective families.

Junor, Penny. *Charles: Victim or Villain*. New York: HarperCollins, 1998.
A veteran royal-watcher portrays Charles as deeply flawed but basically
decent. Diana, also portrayed sympathetically, comes across as an even
more seriously damaged personality.

———. *The Firm: The Troubled Life of the House of Windsor*. New York:
St. Martin's Press, 2005. Junor looks at the Windsor clan after Diana's
death, tracing private and public dysfunctions to their historical roots.

Hounam, Peter, and Derek McAdam. *Who Killed Diana?* Berkeley, CA:
Frog Ltd., 1998. The authors emphasize unanswered questions and
probe for motives to murder.

King, Jon, and John Beveridge. *Princess Diana, the Hidden Evidence:
How MI6 and the CIA Were Involved in the Death of Princess Diana*.

The authors' compelling depiction of secret assassinations is undercut by wild conspiracy theory.

Rees-Jones, Trevor. *Bodyguard's Story: Diana, the Crash and the Sole Survivor*. New York: Warner Books, 2000. The author basically blames the crash on Dodi al-Fayed, who he says insisted on switching cars and putting Henri Paul behind the wheel.

Simmons, Simone. *Diana: The Last Words*. New York: St. Martin's Press, 2005. The author, who claims to have been Diana's confidante, depicts the princess as an ever-changing and often cruel slave to her emotions and baser impulses.

Whitaker, James. *Charles vs. Diana: Royal Blood Feud*. New York: Dutton, 1993. Whitaker, another journalist who has long covered the royals, uses his inside sources to analyze the doomed marriage as it deteriorated.

Index

Index